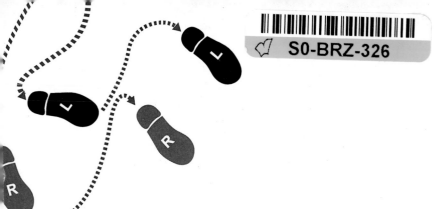

DANCING
WITH THE
TALENT
STARS

25 MOVES THAT MATTER NOW

hcm PRESS

HUMAN CAPITAL MEDIA

"Don't miss this provocative book — it's smart, irreverent and totally resets the talent conversation."

– Steve Arneson, President, Arneson Leadership Consulting and author of *Bootstrap Leadership*

"Essential lessons, insights and tips that could only come from one of the top thought leaders and executives in our profession."

– Ed Betof, Ed.D., Aresty Center Fellow, Wharton Executive Education and author of *Leaders as Teachers* and *Just Promoted!*

"If you are looking for a book that makes a compelling case for all leaders regardless of level to take development seriously, this is it."

– Jack Zenger, CEO, Zenger-Folkman

"Wilde packs his book with the practical insights only learned in the talent management trenches! Put this book on your 'must read' list."

– Marc Effron, President, The Talent Strategy Group and author of *One Page Talent Management*

"This is a brilliant, powerful and easy resource for those committed to talent development at the very highest level."

– Thomas Mungavan, President, and Carol Keers, Vice President, Change Masters Inc.; authors of *Seeing Yourself As Others Do: Authentic Executive Presence At Any Stage Of Your Career*

"Kevin Wilde shows you, in detail, that perfect practice makes positive change and improvement, and makes it permanent!"

– Jack L. Groppel, Ph.D., author, *The Corporate Athlete*

"Reading *Dancing with the Talent Stars* is like taking a master class in talent management."

- Cal Wick, Chairman, Fort Hill Company and author, *Six Disciplines of Breakthrough Learning*

Published by Human Capital Media Press, a division of MediaTec Publishing Inc.

111 E. Wacker Drive, Suite 1290
Chicago, IL 60601
www.humancapitalmediapress.com

ISBN: 978-0-9833712-0-5

"Wilde provides a strong framework of lessons learned ..."

— Wendy L. Lawson, Vice President, Learning and Leadership Development, Discovery Communications

"This book will be a handy tool for entry-level as well as experienced HR professionals."

— Rob Reindl, Corporate Vice President, Human Resources, Edwards Lifesciences

"A great read and a better share."

— Beverly Kaye, Founder and CEO, Career Systems International, co-author of *Love 'Em or Lose 'Em: Getting Good People to Stay*

"*Dancing with the Talent Stars* is not about complicated systems that only a Fortune 100 firm can afford; it's about the everyday things good HR leaders must do."

— David Creelman, CEO, Creelman Research

"A must-have talent management resource."

— Tamar Elkeles, Ph.D., Vice President, Learning and Development, Qualcomm

"A lively, quick read that delivers practical tips on every page."

— Marty Seldman, Executive Coach and co-author of *Survival of the Savvy* and *Executive Stamina*

"*Dancing with the Talent Stars* is a practical, easy-to-apply set of strategic assumptions, frameworks and steps."

— Peter Krembs, Executive Coach and Executive Development Fellow, University of Minnesota Carlson School of Management

"A unique approach to teaching talent professionals everything from learning strategies to communicating with executives."

— Jeffrey A. Berk, Chief Operating Officer, KnowledgeAdvisors

ACKNOWLEDGEMENTS

I've been fortunate to be around many talented stars in my career. Most have been kind enough to take me out on the dance floor of corporate life and teach me some of the right moves. To the executives and HR partners at General Electric and General Mills, thank you for the opportunity to learn from some of the best and be associated with leaders who sincerely value talent development.

To my peer network and external consultants, thank you for coaching me and sharing your lessons learned over the years.

To my sponsors and editors at *Talent Management* and *Chief Learning Officer* magazines, thank you for giving me the opportunity and support to write about my experiences and observations as a practitioner in the field of learning and talent management.

And finally, thank you to my friends and family for the love and encouragement, to my wife Mary who keeps me on my toes and my daughter Sarah who makes me laugh and keeps me moving. Thank you for your discretion in not letting everyone know that I love a good metaphor but am not much on the dance floor.

Kevin D. Wilde

February 2011

TABLE OF CONTENTS

FOREWORD

In the world of consumer products, Wheaties is an iconic brand. "The Breakfast of Champions" has been endorsed by the world's most prominent athletes, from Olympic champions Jesse Owens, Bruce Jenner and Mary Lou Retton to professional stars like Michael Jordan and quarterback Peyton Manning.

But there are a whole different set of champions behind Wheaties: the men and women of General Mills.

While their work isn't recognized on the front of a cereal box, their stamp is evident when you look at the spectacular success of the company. It's those stars behind the scenes who have transformed General Mills from a regional Minnesota mill operator into a global consumer products giant with revenue of more than $19 billion.

More than a manufacturer of world-class products, General Mills is a factory for talent, thanks in large part to the efforts of a true talent management champion, Kevin Wilde. The book you hold in your hand today is the product of his years of experience at two companies renowned for talent development: General Electric and General Mills. Adapted from his regular column in *Talent Management* magazine, this book provides a set of practical, insightful steps to develop your people, your organization and yourself.

Kevin's work has received acclaim from all quarters of the business world. He was named Chief Learning Officer of the Year by *Chief Learning Officer* magazine in 2007. *Training* magazine named General Mills to its respected Hall of Fame in 2010 and *Fortune* recognized the company as one of the top three companies in the world for leadership development.

In addition to *Talent Management*, Kevin's work has been featured in more than two dozen books and magazine articles and quoted by *Bloomberg BusinessWeek*, Financial Times, *Fortune* and *Time* magazine.

Kevin is not only someone whose work I respect. He's also a dear friend who is always willing to lend a hand, no matter how busy he may be. His insight is keen, his perspective simultaneously sharp and nuanced and his generosity unrivaled.

It's my sincere hope that you receive in the following pages even a small portion of the immense insight I've received from one of today's true talent management champions.

Norm Kamikow

President and Editor in Chief, MediaTec Publishing Inc.
February 2011

INTRODUCTION

I've been fortunate to be around stars, and they have all taught me something. Some teach while shining bright; others provide valuable lessons during their ascent or decline. In the past 30 years, my primary job as a practitioner in the field of talent management has been to nurture the stars. The first 17 years of lessons were gleaned during various roles in divisions and corporate settings of General Electric, including some wonderful instructional time at GE's world-renowned corporate development center, Crotonville. The past 13 years have been a journey in transferring the lessons learned to a new setting, General Mills, and charting a new course for talent star growth unique to "The Mills."

Much of what follows is a collection of those talent lessons as first published as "Learning Connections" and "Working Knowledge" columns in *Talent Management* magazine. The 25 lessons presented here are organized by four themes:

- **Talent Management:** Stepping it up to deliver integrated solutions to today's development challenges

- **Learning Strategies:** Providing learning with real performance impact

- **Executive Development:** Grooming executive stars for the main stage

- **HR Excellence:** Assembling a great band of HR teammates for star performance

Each section and chapter begins with a short introduction of the main theme and ends with three thought-provoking next-step questions to help translate the chapter into immediate action. My hope is that you as talent developer, as well as your universe of talent stars, benefit from the ideas and practices presented here.

Kevin Wilde
February 2011

PART ONE
TALENT MANAGEMENT: STEPPING IT UP

With the right steps, promising talent is transformed into star performers. It isn't a random process. The best organizations plan all the right moves for great talent management. First steps include laying in place the right foundation of talent sponsors and aligning the support systems. Skilled footwork is one of the cornerstones of dancing, so being able to set up and conduct a superior talent review is also critical. Organizations realize potential by executing a contemporary balance of developmental actions and systems. While dramatic flourishes grab attention, subtle moves matter as much as large efforts. In talent management, pay attention to the music to keep in step with new trends.

1. LOST AT SEA

Starting up or turning around a talent management practice can often feel like being adrift in an ocean of possibilities and challenges. Where to begin? Where are the stars of today or tomorrow? What are the right first moves that make a difference?

"Lost at Sea" is a classic group exercise in which you imagine being set adrift in a life raft after your ship sinks. The task is to select the essential survival resources from a list of possible resources, from good choices (water, mirror, food rations) to questionable ones (mosquito netting, transistor radio, map of Pacific Ocean). Initial individual selections and team-based rankings are compared to the expert list from the U.S. Coast Guard. The point of the exercise is that a well-crafted team consensus ranking is usually far superior to working alone.

I often receive calls from talent management leaders that remind me of this "Lost at Sea" exercise. The callers are new to the role and are looking for advice on how to start up or turn around a talent management practice. Like the group exercise, the choices are many and it's smart to seek out the collective viewpoints of colleagues.

While I don't work for the U.S. Coast Guard, please allow me to offer my list of essentials. One caution: Context counts, as well as a standard list of smart moves. It's important to understand your surroundings to select the appropriate strategies for your setting. A good choice in one setting may be less than effective in another. With this warning in mind, the following list should apply in most settings.

High-Five List

My top five to build star quality talent in an organization:

1. Sponsors who matter: You can't do it alone no matter how powerful your talent management toolbox. Identify the pro-talent members of the line management staff and cultivate strong relationships. I've been fortunate to have many great line partners over the years, and they have played varied and important roles in the success of talent management efforts. Some are strong advocates for the development changes proposed, and others have helped keep me close to the realities of the business and provided personal mentoring. Some serve as guides to navigate the organization's culture, and others serve as supportive, yet demanding "clients" to solve talent challenges.

2. **A strategic forum to talk talent:** This can be setting up a new meeting, refreshing a stale succession review process or leveraging other avenues by which staffing decisions are made. The aim is to create a strong process that integrates business planning routines with a respected and impactful practice. These sessions have three tangible outcomes:

   1. Firmly link the business plans with the human capital capabilities necessary.

   2. Judge the health of the talent pipeline.

   3. Accelerate the development of potential star talent.

The intangible outcome is to introduce and encourage a talent mindset in line executives. Once you have that value embedded, all the doors open to talent development possibilities.

3. **160-proof rum and shark repellent:** OK, this is from the "Lost at Sea" list, but on stressful days, it may help ease the stress and difficulties that come with improving an organization's talent system. In all seriousness,

> **You can't do it alone, no matter how powerful your talent management toolbox ... so cultivate strong relationships."**

setting a strong talent management agenda is hard work. Resiliency is a prime characteristic of any successful talent champion. Enabling personal support while championing a better way is just as important as any clever talent-building tool.

4. **Strong external network and partners:** Along the lines of "you can't do it alone," introducing or renewing real talent management processes takes good ideas and practical tools. Most of the best tools or processes

I've introduced have originated from a network of great HR mentors and consultants. Whether it was Joe from Utah, Pat from California or Bob from Minnesota, I am indebted to an extended network of great friends and resources. In many cases, they have provided the lifeline of helping me think through a challenge or coming forward with just the right solution. Beyond specific tools and solutions, I've often leveraged the strong and credible voice of outside experts to help influence line managers or existing HR leaders.

5. **Performance management systems that align:** All the parts of HR need to fit, and it's of little lasting value to turbocharge one dimension of HR and not create symmetry and linkage with all other relevant parts. For example, the introduction of a new leadership competency model for training does limited good unless the staffing, measurement and reward systems are also adjusted to the new thinking. Teaching a new leadership capability, such as collaboration, and rewarding individuals for just the opposite has sunk quite a few new development programs. It is imperative to partner with internal HR leaders across the specialties and work as a collective team to serve the business rather than stand out as the lone star of HR excellence.

So it's better to know what to grab when you are faced with a new situation. At sea, that means the right survival gear. To avoid being adrift in the sea of talent management possibilities, it means having a well-tuned set of "can't fail" tools and practices. The strategic talent review is one such tool, but holding the meeting doesn't guarantee success. Adequate preparation, skillful maneuvering in the session and adequate follow-though are the three dimensions to consider.

Next steps:

- Do you have an overall game plan for talent management that incorporates critical elements of identifying, supporting and growing your stars?
- Can you build stronger relationships with the internal sponsors of your talent development efforts?
- How often do you reach out to your external network of fellow talent development practitioners and consultants for ideas and support?

Your next move:

Make the right talent review steps.

2. THE RIGHT STEPS FOR YOUR TALENT REVIEW

Bringing order to talent management means installing useful review processes to keep everyone in step rather than bumping into each other on the dance floor. But to avoid unproductive, ritualistic affairs, prepare well and keep the tempo upbeat in these meetings.

Every day is a talent review day around here. Most days are the informal moments in which the work of talent management usually happens. A decision is made to fill the open sales manager spot with an experienced pro. An impressive presentation is given to a team of senior executives, and the CEO makes a mental note to keep an eye on an up-and-coming marketing director as a high potential.

There are also formal times when we try to bring order and structure to the informality of talent planning and development. Formal events are necessary, as sometimes the daily press of business causes less-than-optimal decisions: the sales slot should be filled by someone with a higher potential profile or the hot-shot marketing director needs a tougher assessment before moving up.

Right Steps for Discussion

There is a collection of right steps, a toolkit of techniques, to inspire useful and productive talent review meetings in which authentic discussion engages line leaders to manage the talent portfolio well. I've learned not to take the success of the discussions for granted. I live by a checklist every year when orchestrating the review. My list to encourage interaction includes:

- **Signal relevance and interaction early.** As you turn to the early topics, there is often a critical moment when an unspoken ground rule is set for participants to "play it safe and not engage" or "join in the fun." It's useful to manage this item early by engineering an interactive topic or inserting questions that signal this is a working session for all.

- **Add something interesting and unexpected.** Break out of the mold of standard HR affairs by sprinkling the agenda with something unique.

Starting the meeting with a slide show with upbeat music about the future; presenting a new scorecard of talent process; and showing a provocative, counterintuitive analysis of talent trends are all ways to inject interest.

- **Coach line leaders to view the talent meetings as important forums to apply their critical thinking and creativity, just as in other working business sessions.** The real value is in the discussion, not the ritualistic review of data or stale facts. Encourage different views and options to talent considerations.

Derailment Up Ahead!

The other checklist I bring into the meeting are "heat of battle" tools to keep things on track, starting with derailment signals. I listen hard to conversations to detect possible trouble ahead. While not all can be uncovered in one meeting, I will probe further when I hear certain problems emerge, such as:

- **A technical star performer with poor team skills:** Results may overshadow interpersonal weaknesses that become more important over time. There are often leaders who perennially leave team problems in their wake as they drive for results.

- **A star in his or her own universe:** This is a promising performer who hasn't really been stretched with new challenges or new settings to advance his or her abilities. A manager can master one job in one set of circumstances but become narrow over time due to the lack of breadth.

- **Yesterday's star with mediocre or declining results today:** Sometimes managers are in a role too long and lose their edge to produce fresh solutions to new challenges. This is usually time to ask about finding a different, revitalizing job for the incumbent and look for the best "trade up" replacements.

Greater Potential Up Ahead

The opposite of confronting derailment is digging for unappreciated or underdeveloped talent. Sometimes executives underplay these up-and-coming managers as a way of hoarding talent. Occasionally the performer's style may not sync well with the manager and he or she is underappreciated for the talent possessed. Three of my favorite potential "accelerators" include:

- **Can see around the corner:** This is the leader who receives high marks for getting out in front of an issue or opportunity before it is present. Sometimes it takes the form of anticipating a problem or setting a vision for his or her team that becomes the right direction over time.

- **Unusual organization savvy:** This leader has the uncanny ability to rally resources across organizational boundaries or can cut through divisional barriers to produce results.

- **Talent magnet and builder:** Special leaders draw in talent and launch an unusual amount of the organization's high potentials. A careful look at nine-block data or backup charts often point to leaders who attract the best and groom the next generation.

Top Questions

To keep the conversation flowing, I've seen leaders unlock insights with great starter questions, such as:

- If we were to put that person in the new role, why would he or she succeed?

- What factors might contribute to failure? How can we engineer the right support for success?

- Given these two candidates for succession, how would we summarize their critical strengths and shortcomings? What would they need to demonstrate to increase our confidence in their capabilities to move up?

- What are the other succession options if this plan proves unrealistic? What can we do now to increase our options down the road?

Good talent management balances the informal, day-to-day actions with the discipline of formal review days. The right steps and interactive techniques spark conversation, check for derailment and uncover unappreciated talent. Furthermore, keep in mind that follow-up actions need to have a contemporary view of your portfolio of star development: assignments, mentoring and formal learning. The old view of this portfolio, often called 70/20/10, can be as stale and out of place as an out-of-date dance step.

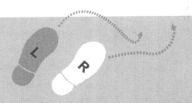

Next steps:

- Have you communicated the strategic link of talent review to your other critical business forums, such as long-range and annual operating planning cycles?

- Can you increase the preparation of line leaders to have real conversations about talent vs. boring forms and data reviews that often deaden talent review meetings?

- How powerful is your "live" toolkit to facilitate talent meetings that uncover derailment, recognize stars in the making and unlock creative development actions?

Your next move:

Refresh your thinking on the right development mix and put old notions to rest.

3. IN MEMORIAM: 70/20/10

The mix we need to grow stars is made up of high-quality job assignments, mentoring and formal learning. Like keeping disco-era moves in contemporary dance routines, an old-fashioned view of the talent mix is out of step with the power of today's development tools.

There is an oft-cited ratio in the field of talent management: 70/20/10. It's really past its prime and needs to be put to rest.

This old ratio is based on a Center for Creative Leadership (CCL) study conducted 30 years ago, asking a small group of executives to recall their most significant development. The researchers reported that 70 percent described on-the-job experiences, 20 percent pointed to relationship-based growth and 10 percent cited formal learning such as classroom training. It made a relevant point back then that we shouldn't only think of development as a training program.

It has since unintentionally morphed into something else. It is common to attend a conference and hear someone describe a strategy for talent development as the old ratio. Everyone in the room nods in recognition of this conventional wisdom. It's not a strategy, and actually, it is now on the level of urban myth – such as the one about the Great Wall of China being visible from outer space. (Sorry, NASA reports it isn't recognizable from space.)

More Fuzzy Than Good Math

The old ratio isn't a strategy and isn't very useful. It is a perfect example of HR-speak that reinforces the jargon-laden, fuzzy-headed label some give our profession. How would you operationalize the old ratio? Does that mean you dedicate 70 percent of your budget to on-the-job training and only 10 percent to structured learning? Does it mean you apportion the amount of executive time devoted to talent development plans exactly to the old ratio?

Any Job Isn't Learning

The 70/20/10 ratio overstates the role of experience in development. The 70 percent can mislead people into thinking as long as everyone is on the job, everyone is developing. Consider the story of two equally qualified candidates vying for the same position. The hiring manager confidently selected one person, even though both had an equal 10 years in their prior roles. The hiring manager deduced that one candidate had 10 years of rich, varied learning, while the other had only one year of learning and repeated the same lessons for nine years.

There's no guarantee that being on the job produces real growth in and of itself. The old ratio may seduce some to think that any job produces development, so talent just needs to stay put and season awhile longer – or worse, the urgent open job is always the right choice for someone's critical next-step development. The reality is that it takes hard work and risk to manage talent development through job assignments.

Three-Martini Lunch Networks

The old ratio understates the value of learning from others. When the first study was done, Ronald Reagan was president, the country club was the predominant community you built and social networking was the three-martini lunch you had with the boys at Harry's. Things moved a lot slower and were more local then, so as long as you could work the internal hierarchy, there was little to be gained by building relationships laterally and outside your organization. Of course, it was harder to connect and learn back then. In the disco era, sending a fax was a big deal and the daily mail was the primary communication mode. The Internet was nonexistent.

> **Use all the contemporary development methods to engage, inform and build talent.**

Classroom as Prison

If social learning was difficult as a development tool 30 years ago, imagine the pain of classroom learning. The standard format for corporate training then was five to 10 days of lecture, usually at a university with academic professors expounding theory X and theory Y using overhead transparencies. If you were lucky, a consultant might show a 35mm film or a slide show to spice things up. Case studies dragged managers through the likes of the history of the Swiss watch industry. These learning opportunities were more rites of passage than relevant, performance-oriented training. No smart, flexible e-learning. No focused events with apply-it-now material.

Consider New Math

Things are different now: Old ratios based on historical realities may not apply neatly. Experience can still be powerful, but needs to be coupled with more precise thinking and discipline. Social networking and informal learning are rising as new modes of knowledge and skill building. Classroom learning has evolved in many ways to be more relevant, more compelling and more accessible on your desktop.

There have been a few attempts to redo the original CCL study, each of them finding different ratios. Let's go beyond the superficial formulas when we consider talent formation strategy. If you do need a number model, here's my 1-2-3 approach. Great talent development is one part focus on the jobs and people that matter most to the business strategy; two parts disciplined review of assessment and calibration with the rigor of financial budgeting; and three parts using contemporary developmental methods to engage, inspire, inform and build talent. Of course, stars hidden or held back rarely shine as brightly as when talent is shared freely throughout an organization to make a greater impact and accelerate development in fresh circumstances.

Next steps:

- Have you educated the organization on an up-to-date view of the proper mix of assignments, mentoring and formal learning?

- Can you improve the value of on-the-job learning by aligning the nature of the work with the competencies and experiences most important for the talent to grow?

- Are you deploying the latest tools to leverage social learning, mentoring and dynamic formal learning in your organization?

Your next move:

Develop ways to move developing stars around.

4. SHARING TALENT

Rising stars are too often hidden or locked up in one corner of the organization. This may maximize value to the current boss, but it under-leverages the impact and growth potential of the employee. It takes extra effort to break free from organizational gravity and self-interest to move your best around.

I wasn't in the room for my first performance appraisal, but I later found out about a "development opportunity" I could have used to improve. Years later, this mistake is all too common in growing today's talent.

My first appraisal happened when Mrs. Kay, my kindergarten teacher, told my parents that I was a bright, energetic 5-year-old who didn't sleep at nap time and had some trouble sharing. While I've overcome the inability to nap during the day, I still have to remind myself to share my best toys.

The Need for Greed

If Mrs. Kay were appraising business leaders today, she would give low marks for sharing high-potential leadership talent. Of course, it's a challenge to convince executives to move their most promising personnel to other parts of the enterprise. Great talent produces great results. Why would a leader give up a valued producer, especially someone with the promise of delivering even greater results in the future?

Executives invest in their high potentials and deserve to reap the benefits. Rational business leaders are unwilling to give up their best in exchange for someone else's so-called high potentials. It feels like a risky, unfair trade to give up talent you know for an unknown. Faced with this risk, it is common for a leader to dig in his or her heels and not share. Worse yet, leaders sometimes hide their best talent, lest corporate finds out about the rising star.

Share to Gain

Now, as any kindergarten teacher would know, there is much to be gained by sharing. Any one business unit can offer job growth and stretch assignments. But at some point, new job challenges in the division aren't as strong or as optimal as those outside the familiar unit. New business circumstances, new geography and new challenges broaden leadership capabilities. Moreover, moving talent across the silos of the organization generates benefits. Fresh high-potential leaders moving into a new group often raise the performance standards and recalibrate expectations to higher levels. Mixing the best talent will bring new thinking and best-practice sharing with accelerated application. These folks are, by nature, change agents.

It makes all the sense in the world to liberate developing leaders to move across business units. While it is hard work, I've observed a number of enablers to better talent sharing.

- **Corporate Ownership**
  Start by declaring that above a certain level, the leadership group is owned by the corporation and not the sole property of the individual business units. Establish that the career development of the top 100, 500 or 1,000 leaders will have a company point of view. It may not be a popular message, but it makes sense when you consider how succession, compensation and development line up to treat leaders beyond a certain level as corporate assets who are on loan to a division.

- **Talent Identification**
  Build into any succession roll-up a robust process to identify and track the best talent in the organization's silos. The CEO and senior team should know the up-and-coming talent, first through this annual HR system but also by taking time to meet and build relationships with each division's high potentials. This can facilitate movement. Sometimes cross-divisional moves happen naturally, and sometimes it takes more. I've seen development-oriented CEOs personally intervene to rescue emerging executives who are being held hostage in a greedy division.

- **Pocketbook Management**
  One of the natural ways the corporation manages the top group of leaders is through its direct ownership of their compensation. Merit pay, stock options, incentive pay and other forms of rewards are often managed at the top for divisional leaders. This practice can be useful in cross-division talent movement by reinforcing the belief that the corporation has a say in the treatment of these leaders. Reviews can be useful assessment and tracking practices to know where the best talent is located in divisions.

- **Educational Events**
  Training can play a role in identifying and enabling the cross-business

movement of high-potential talent, as well. Filling a corporate leadership development program with high potentials from all corners of the organization is a smart way to identify the best divisional talent. The networking from this mixture alone can help open up possible cross-unit movement. Add in direct and meaningful contact with the CEO and other corporate leaders to reinforce the visibility and relationship. Finish by sending the message that the leadership development path to the top will be built with broad, cross-business executive moves.

- **Slate Setting**
  If you can establish that the corporation owns the top leadership group in each division, then it is logical that the corporate office will be involved in filling the leadership jobs in that division. The role can vary, from helping assemble the slate of candidates to reviewing the finalists. The aforementioned enablers set the stage for this kind of role. This is the critical time to nudge a division executive to consider a high potential from another unit or recruit a talented person from another division to interview for the opening.

Leadership development research reminds us that challenging assignments are the accelerators of growth. At some point in a leader's journey, new horizons of development are found in crossing divisions and not staying in the home unit. It takes courage and clarity of purpose to align all talent owners to the bigger view of star development. Likewise, it takes clarity of thinking to ensure all leaders understand what a star is and how to best communicate that potential.

Next steps:

- How can you bring a "share to gain" mindset to your business leaders to grow and redeploy developing talent?

- Which enabler would increase the flow of talent across organizational boundaries: increased corporate ownership, talent identification, compensation practices, training events or slate setting?

- How can you structure your tracking and talent review systems to increase the visibility of emerging talent to a wider audience?

Your next move:

Don't get your communication wrong and leave great talent on the roof.

5. IS YOUR TALENT ON THE ROOF?

Stars need to know their standing in the organization. Unfortunately, most organizations have a confused view about whether they should inform talent about their potential to grow and advance. Fortunately, there's a simple move to learn with only three different steps to consider. From there, it's practice, practice, practice.

There is an old story of a vacationer calling his house sitter to determine if everything was OK at home.

"Everything is fine, but I'm sorry to say your favorite cat Fluffy died," the house sitter reported in an unsympathetic, matter-of-fact tone.

"Oh no, that's terrible news ... and you shouldn't be so direct in telling me," replied the distraught homeowner. "Break it to me slowly. First tell me Fluffy is up on the roof. Then next time I call, tell me the cat is off the roof but caught a bad cold. Then on the third call, tell me you took Fluffy to the vet and my pet couldn't be saved."

"Now, tell me, how is grandma?"

There was a pause, and then the house sitter replied, "Oh, she's fine ... but grandma is on the roof right now!"

Telling the Truth About Potential

So often our work in HR is confronting challenging situations and communicating tough messages. Unfortunately, we often confuse people by being too obtuse or avoiding difficult conversations altogether. In the world of talent management, we are most conflicted about whether to inform employees about their potential.

This ambiguity about telling is unfortunate and has adverse consequences. High-potential employees are romanced away by other firms because they don't know the bright future they have with their present employer. Learning about it while trying to resign brings the employer's credibility into question. On the other hand, good performers obsessing about their potential label can be a distraction and can destroy teamwork. Some may have inflated expectations of rapid advancement without benefiting from the critical lessons of the current role. When HR isn't clear on the right position or inconsistent across the enterprise, it reinforces the perception that HR is soft-headed and fragmented.

The Landing Spots

So let's get clear on this whole telling thing. First, recognize you can only select one of three positions. They are:

- **Closed position:** Ignore the question of potential and keep employees focused on today's work.

- **Open position:** Regularly inform all employees about how the organization judges their future.

- **Half-open position:** A legitimate middle position, as long as it is thoughtfully considered and well-executed. There are two variations: Inform some people of their standing, but not all. This is to be strategically transparent to certain employee populations, such as fast-track development participants or critical capability pipeline people. The other option is to tell all employees some things about potential but not engage in full disclosure. For example, you might be general about advancement opportunities or timing of a person's move.

The Guidelines

So what's the right choice for your organization? Three questions point to the right position:

1. Are you confident in the call? Can your managers make quality calibration judgments? Are your nine-blocks more the work of fiction, or real assessments of who is capable of greater roles? Is the distinction between performance and potential clearly understood? Do your managers have a good handle on what the critical needs are for future roles? Are your talent succession discussions – the collective calibration – rigorous and regular enough?

> **We are conflicted about whether to inform employees about their potential ... often with unfortunate consequences.**

2. Is it useful for employees to know? Will employees benefit from knowing? In an aggressive, performance-oriented culture, employees should know their prospects. Should their energy be spent getting ready to move up or move out? Likewise, will the organization benefit from a talent pool in a constant state of churn as a way of keeping fresh, or would the organization benefit from retained organizational knowledge and steady, team-oriented performers? Does the "tell" position align with your reward scheme?

3. Can the message be delivered well? To what degree can managers deftly inform employees about their potential? I once worked with an executive who was so bad at communicating the right message that our best talent often left his office thinking their career was coming to an end. We finally learned to automatically schedule a recovery meeting with HR every time a high potential went to visit the executive.

Good Talent-Sitting

As the talent sitters for the organization, we shouldn't be muddled about communicating potential. Figure it out and get on with it. Take the position of telling if your managers can make good judgments, can inform employees well and transparency is useful to the employee and the organization. If you can't respond as confidently in these three aspects, take a more conservative closed or part-open position. For some, taking a firm stand on communicating potential is a big step, and for others, it's a small move. Don't discount the value of small moves that add up over time.

Next steps:

- Do you have a clear view on the current practice of informing talent throughout your organization? Is it consistent and well-understood?

- In reviewing the three factors of organizational context – confidence in the call, employee usefulness, delivery quality – is your current practice well-aligned or should you consider changing?

- How can you work to improve these three organization context factors to increase the transparency of potential to your talent?

Your next move:

Nano-talent moves matter, too.

6. NANO-TALENT MOVES

Champions on the dance floor know that impressive routines are often composed of a series of small, well-executed steps that form an extraordinary performance. Likewise, consistently focusing on small improvements in talent development routines hold as much promise as any large-scale change program.

Think small, as well as big. We are often drawn to the large initiative, the enterprise-wide change effort and the big, hairy, audacious goal. But save some room for the nano-moves. Nano-moves are smoother, reasonable moves in the spirit of kaizen: small changes, made daily, that over time compound into a significant improvement.

To get you started, I've listed 12 ideas. You can add your own to the list, or better yet, pull group together to brainstorm a master list of nano-moves. Then pull out your calendar and block out a small amount of time each day, week or month to apply a move.

'Support Someone' Moves

1. **Broker a new mentoring relationship with a high potential or expat.** Look at your "talent on the move" lists and find two people who would benefit from each other's wisdom. Make the inquiry today to set up an introductory meeting.

2. **Help someone get off the derailment track.** It's all too common to see promising talent in a stretch role derail, often due to lack of honest feedback and support. Encourage the manager or HR generalist of a wavering employee to provide the message – in a caring and direct fashion – followed by the right resources and needed training.

3. **Show love to one of your best.** Initiate a meaningful retention effort to someone you are counting on growing in your star factory. Let a high potential know how much he or she means to your organization and how bright the future is before an external recruiter spins tales of greener pastures.

4. **Welcome the new recruit after the fact.** The initial rush of on-boarding usually propels new employees in the right direction. There is often a morale dip after six months, what I call reality check time. Check in with someone with six-month tenure to see how he or she is doing and how you can help.

> **Save some room for the nano — smoother, reasonable moves — as well as for the big, hairy, audacious goals.**

'Make Room' Moves

5. **Find something to stop doing.** We all fall in the trap of maintaining yesterday's legacy programs while stuffing in all the new work of talent development. Make room for the new, or at least give yourself breathing room by reducing. Likely candidates? Try the bottom end of a fresh ranking of the highest-impact talent efforts. At a minimum, hit the pause button on something for three months and see if anyone notices.

6. **Streamline and simplify the grand old program.** It was launched with such grandeur and enthusiasm awhile back. But now you can get by with a little less overhead. Revisit the core purpose and challenge yourself to redesign it with half the resources.

'Build Yourself' Moves

7. **Go learn more about the business.** Buy a line leader coffee or host a lunch to dive deeper into his or her operations and challenges. A recent study reported that the No. 1 factor to an HR professional's success is the amount of business acumen. Add to yours today.

8. **Chat with an expert.** Enjoy a post, article or book lately? Most authors of books or blogs are happy to respond to brief requests from readers. Reach out to let them know you enjoyed their writing and would like to spend a minute or so chatting more about a key idea. You can do the same with conference speakers or consultants.

9. **Learn from a winner.** Notice all those "best of" magazine lists and

professional group awards in the talent field? Why not learn more about an excellence practice by contacting a winner and hearing more about the inside story. Also, reach out to the people who put the list together to discover the overall findings and practical applications.

A Few More Moves

10. **Invite an internal executive to one of your training programs.** Even a short segment taught by an insider has greater credibility in the classroom – physical or virtual – than an external trainer, and it encourages the teaching leader to keep growing too.

11. **Thank someone for his or her help in your talent development efforts.** Send a quick e-mail, text, tweet or call to recognize someone's contribution. Gratitude has a way of making a difference in ways seen and unseen.

12. **Seek a small dose of feedback on something you are doing.** Use the rule of three here: Ask three people (program participant, HR partner, line sponsor). Pose three simple questions: What's working? How is it helping? How can it be better?

Benchmarking the best in the talent management field can often be a humbling experience. But the secret in stellar star-development systems can be found in small and consistent improvements. "Kaizen" is an old word with current relevance to the development field, and it signals as important a trend as any hot new practice in the field.

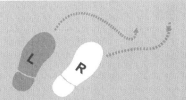

Next steps:

- Are there simple ways you can increase the support to your most important talent?

- What are a few low-value-producing practices ripe for retirement to free up time and resources for something fresh?

- How can you add to your personal toolkit with simple steps to learn more about the business or from the best in the talent field?

Your next move:

Talent management is a dynamic and forward-moving field, so it's important to keep your terms and talent dictionary up to date.

7. THE NEW TALENT MANAGEMENT DICTIONARY

Knowing the right moves today means knowing the modern terms for the moves. By doing a bit of stargazing, the future of talent development becomes clearer as new words signal the trends of tomorrow.

To the editors of the Oxford English Dictionary:
With each new edition of your esteemed publication, you introduce entirely new words or interesting uses for existing words. I have a few nominations for next year's edition.

In researching your procedure, I've learned that you employ 50 readers to search all types of contemporary printed material for word candidates. Also, you apply a five-year rule between a word's first appearance and when its coinage signifies sustaining currency vs. a short-term fad.

Let me save your editors some time and effort. I believe the words that follow will become commonplace in the next five years and signify important trends in the field of talent management.

New Talent Words

Care bear: The insatiable demand for feedback and validation from the millennial generation causes organizations to designate full-time positions to dole out coaching and support, regardless of reporting relationship.
Usage: "Oliver is feeling a lot better now that he's reconnected with his care bear."

Gray ceiling: An artificial career advancement barrier for younger workers created by the delay in retirement of baby boomers.
Usage: "Kate's promotion is a rare break in the gray ceiling around here."

Helicopter promotion: Parents of millennials continue to be overly involved in their children's lives, even hovering over their adult working careers. HR departments cave into the pressure and start granting promotions based on parental lobbying rather than employee merit.

Usage: "The latest marketing moves can only be explained as helicopter promotions."

High-mob leader: Short for high-mobility leader. A new nine-block arrays a firm's talent pipeline by performance and willingness to relocate.

Usage: "While she won't set the world on fire, high-mob Terry is willing to move to general manager job in Istanbul."

Minute-clinic coach: First seen at the Mall of America, kiosks spring up in malls across the country, where local consulting firms offer speedy career counseling to corporate types taking a break from shopping.

Usage: "Mike is trying a new influence tactic he picked up last week at the South Town minute-clinic coach."

Pipe-fitter: Talent stolen from another company to rebuild a weak talent pipeline. Many organizations can't respond to the growth opportunities of the economic recovery due to the lack of internal "ready now" leaders and instead aggressively pirate promising talent from their competitors.

Usage: "John's arrival as the latest talent pipe-fitter brought new energy and three additional recruits into the new business venture."

Plug-ins: Seminar reception and social networking time is replaced by gatherings in which participants recharge their smart phones and laptops rather than mingling (see thumbinar).

Usage: "I barely made it to the afternoon conference plug-in as my iPhone battery was down to 1 percent power!"

> **These words will be commonplace in the next five years and signify important trends in the field of talent management.**

Re-fo consultant: A refocused consulting practice. Reversing the trend of consolidation in the talent management consulting field, firms dismantle the odd collection of acquisitions that never found much cross-practice synergy and often confused clients.

Usage: "Irene is a lot more effective as a re-fo consultant rather than fronting for the old GAS-E (general advice services - enterprise) conglomerate."

Thumbinar: A seminar in which it is permissible for participants to keep thumbs actively working their smart phones, constantly checking e-mail, Facebook and Twitter during presentations (see plug-ins).

Usage: "MediaTec broke new ground with its latest Talent Management thumbinar by having presenters post tweets every five minutes to keep the audience engaged."

TMS/LMS app: Complete talent and learning management systems operated from a handheld iPhone or BlackBerry. The 99-cent version of what were once large-scale software systems allow talent managers and HR departments to provide workforce planning, training and knowledge management services at the touch of a thumb.

Usage: "Let me check my iPhone TMS app to get you a list of candidates for that global sales VP position."

OZ time: In the demanding always-on global work environment, employees are expected to be engaged 24/7, except when applying out-of-zone benefit time (OZ time). OZ time replaces vacation, holiday and sick time granted to employees and is used to designate hours not available.

Usage: "Mary catches up on her sleep by applying most of her OZ time this year between midnight and 5 a.m."

Next steps:

- What are the new ways to support emerging stars from today's generation?
- How can the new ways of learning and development be deployed in your organization to increase experimentation?
- What new words and phrases have you heard lately that may signal intriguing possibilities for your talent development practice?

PART TWO
LEARNING STRATEGIES: PRACTICE MAKES PERFECT

What distinguishes great talent and stars on the rise? Their pace in learning and improving. By definition, potential is about something detected yet unproven: the ability to achieve high levels of impact and take on increased scope and scale in responsibilities. But run-of-the-mill classroom dance instruction doesn't unleash top performance.

Strong learning practices make the difference. Smart organizations invest consistently in learning, master the essential moves, ensure that what is taught transfers and use partners well for superior performance.

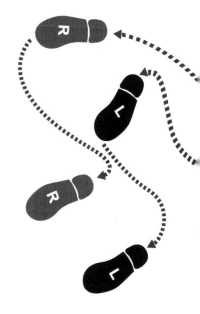

8. A YEAR WITHOUT LEARNING

One partner always leads on the dance floor, and the other follows. While signaling the next step, the skillful lead needs to have the full routine in mind for ultimate success. Knowing where you are headed and how to get there is a prerequisite to lead. Leaders who move while staring down at their feet can negotiate today's demands but will stumble sooner or later.

"This is going to have to be a different story next year," the CEO thought as he wrapped up his report to the board for the fiscal year. "I've guided the corporation through a difficult period. Not as dire as in other industries, but I made some tough calls the board should appreciate.

"Take training. While the complete ban I imposed was unpopular, it did save dollars and time.

Freed from new product and skills training, the sales force could spend more time with customers. The scary-smart talent in R&D stayed in the labs inventing, not out at conferences networking for new ideas – same with our marketing staff. Their training and conference budget was cut to nil.

"Newly promoted managers didn't bother senior executives with mentoring meetings, so my execs could focus on work and let the cream rise to the top like the old days. Business teams throughout the company got to work. They didn't sit around contemplating esoteric topics such as ethics and inclusion."

Explain Away the Numbers

The CEO's self-satisfied glow began to fade as uneasiness crept in. Rereading the numbers portion of the year-end results, he wondered how to explain it to the board.

Market share was down five points. The sales force did have more face time with customers, but its effectiveness wasn't impressive. In fact, comments from the CEO of one of the company's most important customers were concerning. The sales team botched the proposal and let the competition come in at the last minute and steal the contract. Something about misreading the client's real needs.

In defense of the sales force, it really didn't have anything that revolutionary to sell this year. For some reason, the pipeline of new products thinned out.

"But I can't be hard on the R&D leader either," the CEO thought. "Marketing really dropped the ball, missing new trends, and we were blindsided with that new product announcement from our key competitor. I guess the high level of turnover and churn in marketing this past year kept that group in turmoil."

He glanced at the resignation letter on his desk, the latest defection of promising marketing talent.

"I don't understand this new generation," he thought. "Leaving for a role where she felt more commitment to her professional growth, even if the salary and responsibilities aren't that different!

"Those losses have put our new product platform launch behind six months. It's not like I don't give these new leaders visibility. How do I explain to the board the two bright international leaders they met last year are now gone as well?"

The next line of the CEO's report seemed to promise a better story. Head count and overhead expenses were down, below target levels. Defections during the past two years really helped the bottom line for sales, general and administration costs. In fact, no department in the company has a full staff right now. HR seems to take longer and longer to find new recruits.

"I don't know what to make of HR's complaint that our 'employment proposition' isn't compelling enough to attract top talent any more.

"I'm starting to get uneasy that some managers may grab whatever talent comes in the door and the new recruits aren't hitting the ground running like they used to. They're 'C' players."

> **It's been 'C' performance here. We survived, but I'm not sure we are ready to grow. Next year is going to have to be different.**

'C'-Level Performance

"That's about right," he thought. "It's been 'C' performance here. We survived, but I'm not sure we are ready to grow. Next year is going to have to be different. It's clear we'll have to make some bold decisions to turn this around. We'll have to have the courage to make some new strategic investments.

"The sales force will need to gain competence in front of customers. R&D will need to get out more to challenge traditional thinking and bring more innovation. Marketing also will have to get out more, and senior leaders have to carve time out to help the next generation feel valued and pass along lessons of experience so we can do a better job retaining our top talent and regaining our reputation.

"There hasn't been much formal training around here lately," the CEO concluded, "but maybe I did learn something valuable. Learning investments are important and the essentials matter."

Next steps:

- How can you keep reminding top leaders of the value of training investments for short-term performance and longer-term success?

- What are ways to increase external focus, internal cross-division collaboration and innovation through formal learning initiatives?

- Are you sure the best talent and rising stars receive adequate development investments for retention and accelerated growth?

Your next move:

Master the learning fundamentals.

9. THREE ESSENTIALS FOR LEARNING

Good technique is evident as couples move effortlessly across the dance floor. Footwork, posture and turning are just three of the many skills to be mastered. In organizations, star-caliber learning happens when three essentials are equally grasped: purpose, support and outcomes. Talent leaders who pay attention to these fundamentals capture the full value of learning investments.

There comes a time in every learning professional's life when you are faced with heading back to the drawing board or scheduling the celebration party. Lately, I've been thinking about the difference between getting something right and getting a do-over. After nearly 30 years in the development field, it seems to me that good work boils down to three simple questions:

- What am I trying to do?
- Who cares?
- How will I know I've been successful?

When the answers to these questions ring true, you probably have a winner on your hands. When the responses are unclear, you'll find yourself asking, "Why did I ever do that?"

What Am I Trying to Do?

Learning and development efforts live in the land of good intent. We want to help and add value. The trap is anything that sounds like a request for help and smells like smoke. It rings an alarm to send the training fire truck to put out the fire. Sometimes, in our haste, we forget to confirm the address of the burning building.

There have been times in the middle of implementing a training program when I wished I asked more questions upfront. Too often, there is a quick jump to a solution, a drive to get in motion and a desire to not appear slow.

One of the most successful executives I ever worked with said, "The times in my career when I had the most trouble were when I didn't know exactly what I wanted." It's important to be clear when considering learning as a response to what is needed.

To dig deeper into knowing exactly you want, ask questions such as:

- What does success look like?
- What's the gap between the situation and desired performance?
- If we do this, what will happen?

Who Cares?

Participants are the first group to ask, "Who cares?" This question is the core of motivation and engagement, and answering it can make a critical difference. We've all sat in a classroom or attended a webcast only to become distracted or apathetic.

> **When I forget to walk in the learner's shoes, I find myself leading an elegantly designed learning parade without any followers.**

Great learning is grounded firmly in the point of view and the motives of the participants, such as the new employee trying to get traction in new surroundings, the experienced manager grappling with another round of corporate initiatives or the up-and-coming executive stretching to succeed in an expatriate assignment.

Walking in the learners' shoes makes an incredible difference. When I forget, I find myself leading an elegantly designed learning parade without anyone following.

Once the link between learner motivation and a training offering is established, consider other stakeholders. "Who cares?" can be aimed at the learner's manager, who is often the biggest leverage link missed. Before heaping tasks on learners' managers, first understand how they will benefit from improved performance.

Also, consider team members who can provide support to learners. Senior leaders can signal the value of the learning program, contribute resources and, best of all, they can be visible role models for learning.

How Will I Know?

Clear answers to the first two questions are usually the transition point from inquiry to action. I've learned to pause and dig deeper with another question. How do I know the results have been achieved?

It's difficult to put time and energy into the hard work of evaluation when the next unmet learning need calls. But if learning is about positive change and making a difference, then skipping evaluation is not an option.

Evaluation requires linking back to the first two questions on intended impact. Reinforce the learning through a follow-up process that actually begins upfront – looping back to key stakeholders to talk about assessing impact and accountability before starting the big program.

Following up is also a way to continue the learning. I ask participants to assess progress against their original improvement goals and determine what new tools or learning resources are needed to encourage a next step. I also ask direct managers to evaluate impact and encourage them to provide additional coaching or encouragement.

Choose Your Essentials

As simple as these three questions are, better learning connections ensue when you use them. When I forget or do a superficial job attending to my big three, I find myself going back to the drawing board. So whether you are facing the do-over drawing board or starting to design on a fresh canvas, I encourage you to apply the essentials first.

Next steps:

- How can you ensure clarity of purpose before committing to a training solution?

- Have you secured appropriate levels of support and sponsorship for the training ahead?

- Are you reserving an appropriate amount of focus and resources to assess if your training purpose has been achieved?

Your next move:

Bridge lessons to on-the-job application or risk the flood of reality.

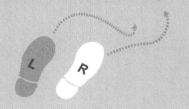

10. LEARNING BEFORE THE FLOOD

Sometimes you can go through the motions of training but not commit to applying the learning later. The music doesn't feel right, you can't get the beat and that pivot turn isn't working out. When it counts, even well-intended instructional programs face challenges to transfer lessons learned into practice. Overcoming the learning vs. doing gap requires resetting the expectations of all involved and engineering innovative approaches.

The hurricane ravaged the New Orleans area with sustained winds of 120 miles per hour, rain poured down up to 20 inches in some areas and the surge topped the levees meant to protect the region. The havoc forced 1 million people to be evacuated, and it destroyed 600,000-plus buildings.

A report on Hurricane Katrina? No, this was the opening of a U.S. Federal Emergency Management Agency (FEMA) press release one year before Katrina, describing a five-day planning exercise with emergency officials from 50 parish, state, federal and volunteer organizations. Their purpose was to learn how to coordinate a quick response to a catastrophic hurricane in Louisiana.

What followed in August 2005 was the real thing. Little evidence exists that there was much application from the FEMA workshop. While most of us provide lessons of a much different kind, we all too often share the frustration of having little on-the-job application to show for the training provided.

Just on Vacation

The issue is called "transfer." Whether it's failing to apply lessons from a classroom, an e-learning program or even a live simulation, it is the most challenging aspect of formal development.

Over the years, I've observed that each party in a development effort misreads the assigned role.

- **The participant:** Trouble begins when training lacks relevance and a participant treats a workshop as vacation: "Just here for the food and sights, with not much to take back except for a few good memories." Likewise, rushing through an e-learning module as one clears junk from an overloaded e-mail inbox fails to provide much benefit. Of course, we infrequently set up learning events with the expectation of accountability for the learner or the direct manager.

- **The manager:** While most will want a fully trained employee, managers often fail to support the training opportunity. They treat it as nothing more than scheduling an employee absence – just like a vacation. But rarely is the manager asked to do more to leverage learning, primarily due to the lack of contact with the learning and development (L&D) leader.

- **The L&D leader:** I admit to playing vacation planner rather than focusing on performance expectations for participants and managers. The instant gratification that comes from happy learners in the event or positive buzz from an online module provides the premature feeling of a mission accomplished. I miss asking the hard question about whether anything covered was applied later.

> **The value of any development effort is more in the application and impact than in the program itself.**

I am paying attention to transfer more, thanks to a recent field trip.

Lessons From a Field Trip

A simple two-day offering has taught me much about strong transfer back on the job. Called Getting Things Done (GTD), it's a custom version of the popular David Allen Co. time and workflow management training. In observing the impressive impact of this training, I've discovered four principles that enable transfer:

1. **The Field Trip Principle:** Build in time and support for hands-on application during the learning. Most training separates the learning from the application. Most people take a time management class to deal with their mountain of to-do items, not intending to add a new layer of tasks after a class. We designed a stealth application session into the program, in which participants are sent back to their offices or laptops on the second day of the program to start applying the class material.

2. **The Accountability Principle:** Design supportive accountability measures to help the learner follow through. To overcome the temptation of just doing normal office work during the field trip, each participant was intentional in his or her learning by first mapping out which GTD lesson would be applied. Upon returning to the class, participants reported back progress and surprises.

3. **The "Your Enthusiasm Helps" Principle:** Provide coaching and encouragement as lessons are being applied. Post-field trip debrief sessions provide great peer-to-peer teaching and inspiration when participants enthusiastically share their progress and obstacles in first-time application. Seeing someone else apply a lesson with success provides additional confidence and encouragement for further application.

4. **The Stick Around Principle:** Keep following up with support and encouragement over time. We've extended the spirit of the field trip debriefing by offering post-program support, including e-mails with tips and encouragement, as well as leveraging social media to keep learning cohorts together after the event.

Transfer for Value

The value of any development effort is more in the application and impact than in the program itself. The lesson of the FEMA workshop is that worth isn't in the design of the five-day event, but the practical application when the real storm hits.

Avoid falling into the training-as-vacation trap by applying the principles of the field trip to ensure learning transfers to real value on the job. It's an exercise in influence that can be deployed either when learning is optional or when it's required.

Next steps:

- How can you communicate the right role expectations to participants and managers when setting up learning for transfer?
- What ways can you avoid the trap of vacation planner when contracting for training projects?
- Where can the field trip principles of time for application, accountability, peer support and follow-up support be applied in your training efforts?

Your next move:
Ensure good learning and transfer, even when training is mandatory.

11. SOFTENING THE MANDATE

Champions distinguish themselves through their mastery of the compulsory segment of dance competition. In organizations, compulsory or mandatory training rarely elicits much excitement or high levels of performance. Yet, required training can be valuable if a strategy is deployed that moves participants from compliance to commitment.

Mandatory training is one of the most vexing aspects of the learning dance.

Whether it's ethics, diversity, regulatory compliance or the latest culture change, employees often are involved because we make them participate. The intent of mandatory training is honorable. By forcing compliance, however, we violate the most basic rule of learning: Adults seek learning for their reasons, not because they were told.

A few years ago, I was drafted to support a senior leader's dream of a sweeping culture change related to meeting etiquette. The mission handed down to me was: Have the top 1,000 leaders schooled on the new way. I proceeded to engineer a series of learning events, complete with a tight tracking mechanism so no one would escape. The result was an impressive corporate rollout. Less impressive was lasting evidence of improvement. In the end, it was all a waste of time.

From Compliance to Commitment

Our work is influence-based. Social psychologists have studied influence for many years and have classified the tactics thereof as either hard or soft. The difference is the amount of freedom a person exercises to yield or resist a tactic.

Hard tactics are more forceful and push the individual. The result is submission, but that might result in unintended opposition. If you've seen participants show up or log in to your program with low engagement and apathy, you've produced compliance, but not much more. If you've seen avoidance, passive-aggressive behavior or even a bit of sabotage, your influence efforts have gone beyond generating compliance to breeding resistance. Mandated training is clearly a hard tactic. Soft tactics, on the other hand, are actions that produce commitment.

I am fortunate to have a communication offering that needs no CEO mandate. Each program is booked solid for the next 12 months with an extended waiting list. The training fills a need everyone can see. But not all of our work falls into this category. Some mandatory training seems unavoidable to run an enterprise. So what do we do?

> **Adults seek learning for their reasons and not because they are told.**

The starting point is to minimize the learning-by-command rationale. Most senior leaders are willing to listen to the downside of mandatory training. As long as rollout plans are aggressive and promise impact, most leaders will accept training that garners commitment while avoiding the resistance a fiat generates.

But when everyone must go through training, the research on influence points to the need for a mixture of hard and soft tactics. In fact, studies have shown blended influence strategies can double or triple the odds of success.

Consider the Soft Seven

When faced with compulsory training, increase your influence with the following methods.

The first three have the most power to build commitment:

1. **Consultation:** Involve the target audience in planning or choosing how to receive the training.

2. **Inspirational appeal:** Build an emotional request or proposal that arouses positive reaction by appealing to commonly held values and beliefs.

3. **Personal appeal:** Based on your credibility and relationship, ask for participation as a favor.

Moderately effective influence tactics include:

4. **Rational persuasion:** Provide logical arguments and factual evidence to win support.

5. **Integrating:** Get the audience in a good mood before soliciting involvement.

6. Upward appeal: Seek approval of those in higher positions and leverage that approval when communicating.

7. Exchange: Offer a reward or tangible benefit for participation or remind someone of a favor that should be reciprocated.

If I had another shot at rolling out that initiative on meetings, I could augment the hard compliance aspect by first consulting with key stakeholders on delivery options. When soliciting the first wave of participants, I could have the senior sponsor – or other credible supporters in groups where I have a record of good work and strong relationships – provide the emotional appeal to sign up.

Do not be seduced into going for compliance alone. Make more of an effort to gain commitment. The outcome will produce the lasting value-add we all strive to achieve.

Next steps:

- Which training is viewed as mandatory for your participants, and how can you confirm that it is necessary for all?

- Which of the seven influence methods could be applied to an upcoming compulsory training program to increase the commitment vs. simple compliance?

- Is there any current mandatory training that could be redesigned with the seven influence tactics in mind?

Your next move:

To gain commitment, use influence as a powerful tool for change management.

12.

FOR LEARNING YOU'LL LIKE, PRESS SEVEN

The pace of change today requires a willingness to stay in motion, never being settled with the moves you know and ever-ready to take on new steps. On a good day, we are all willing to try a new routine, but we also have days when we yearn to be left alone and shuffle along with well-known, comfortable steps. So how can change and learning be presented in a way that elicits a good-day readiness to try something new?

A wave of pent-up energy was released during a recent staff meeting. We were anticipating the rollout of a new voice-mail system, and the upgrade was causing significant anxiety.

"I just learned how to work the last upgrade, and now I have to start over again!" someone cried. "I can't believe I need a 30-page manual just to get my messages!" another said.

We concluded the discussion by agreeing nothing strikes fear in our hearts more than an announced system update. Feeling good about our venting, we moved on to our next agenda item: a new leadership training program to create change agents. Asking people to learn something new can be tricky, even for those of us who advocate for learning.

Change is something we like to initiate, support and manage, but change done to us is unwanted. What's a learning champion to do?

My Upgrade Is Your Downgrade

First, remind yourself that your announced upgrade is often the learner's perceived downgrade. In the case of the new voice-mail system, my staff members initially focused on what they were losing: control, confidence and competence. Learning a new system would take time and energy that might be spent more productively elsewhere.

First, communicate what remains the same to reinforce that the learner still has control and competence. Then, link the intent of the new effort with established objectives. For example, I remember sitting through the launch of Six Sigma at GE's Crotonville training center and hearing the CEO explain how this new thing would be a logical extension of our good old WorkOut and productivity best practices. What a difference that context made in my acceptance of Six Sigma.

Is There a Reason to Believe?

Second, tap into the right motivational message for your learner. The old saying still applies: "People do things for their reasons, not your reasons." What benefits can you list on the positive side of your learners' balance sheet? Does it solve their problems? Will it help learners achieve performance goals for the year or knock something off their to-do lists?

Beyond solving known problems, will acquiring skills and knowledge add delight? Our unwanted phone system upgrade offered the ability to hear e-mail messages. Once my team members mastered the phone basics, they quickly used this new feature to tame the e-mail beast while they checked voice mail. Now, they love the new system and wouldn't go back to the old one.

> **"Change is something we like to initiate, support and manage, but change done to us is unwanted.**

It's Easy

Third, find ways to make the learning journey convenient. Working in a consumer food company, it's become clear to me that everyone enjoys eating, but few enjoy cooking and cleaning up. It's all about convenience. So our research and development folks find ways to make great-tasting meals and take steps out of the cooking process.

Our advertising professionals stress the product simplicity of "Heat and Eat" and "No Cleanup Required." Does your training feel simple to the user? Are there only a few steps? Is it easy to access and complete without much cleanup?

Reigniting the Flame of Curiosity

Finally, the best way to tip the scales in favor of your program and motivate learners is to tap into their curiosity. Natural curiosity often fades in adulthood — we turn off the curiosity instinct that enabled us to discover new learning. We instead turn our energy to defending the status quo, perceiving anything new as a threat rather than an opportunity to grow.

You can reignite curiosity and growth any number of ways. Encourage learners to identify something they do well now and then reflect back on when they first acquired the skill. Remind them of how they've gotten better at something in the past. Create a spark. Use benchmarking, action learning and best-practice exercises to connect people to what's possible and start them down the path of development.

Take an honest look at the learner's balance sheet of what is gained or lost by change. Ensure the leaner can find new ways to solve problems and achieve objectives. Be sure the overall experience is more fun than frustrating and builds curiosity.

Next steps:

- How can you identify with the learner by considering what is lost as well as gained by change and the new learning required?

- How can you add positives to your learner's balance sheet to tap into internal motivation?

- Can you streamline and simplify lessons for your learners so it's easy and doesn't require unnecessary effort?

Your next move:
Seek out good partners to help you master the moves of change and learning.

13. DANCE WITH GREAT PARTNERS

It takes two to tango. New talent development programs often mean skillfully partnering with external experts. While their star expertise can be clearly seen at the beginning of an engagement, don't take the process of partnering lightly. The internal vs. external connection can lead to unfortunate slip-ups. Done right, dancing with a strong partner can add much to any learning and development initiative. Just watch your step.

He has penned a best-seller. You've written a few memorable e-mails. She has a two-by-two matrix to explain the four types of anything. You have a few rules of thumb that keep you out of trouble. He gets paid a lot to explain his hot new theory of management. You get paid by the month.

Yes, that famous consultant is coming to your organization to give the Big Speech. And while you differ in many ways, you have one thing in common: You both hope the engagement goes well.

I've had the honor and frustration of working with many of these star consultants and their Big Speeches over the years. What I've learned is that engagements can go well if you see it as a dance and master two critical moves.

Before We Dance: Who Leads?

This is the question of partnership. Some star consultants prefer to go it alone, and others will welcome your help with open arms. I call the former "lone stars" and the latter "partner stars."

Lone stars are like this reference I heard recently: "He is quick to expand his activities beyond the agreed-upon base. Once in the organization, he will try to establish a direct relationship with the CEO and in the process, cut out HR."

On the other hand, here's how a partner star sees his role: "I know my responsibility as an outside consultant is to deliver an excellent training session, but it's also to make the internal HR job in managing me as easy as possible and to make them look great."

Both types of stars are welcome in my organization. The partner stars are welcome to stay, and the lone stars are welcome to leave as soon as possible.

I try to set up the partner stars for a successful visit by carefully navigating three topics.

First, let's get clear on expectations. What is the star to deliver? Why do we need it and what does success look like?

While tempted to cover these topics quickly, I find that partner stars really want to know how to craft their material to best fit your need. Trusted partner stars can provide the objective point of view on an important issue that insiders can't offer. Lone stars will listen politely to your briefing and deliver the canned pitch.

> **So when the music starts playing … it's best to figure out who is going to take you around the dance floor.**

Second, let's cover the context. Knowing the dance floor well allows the star to be at her best. I'll pass along relevant information on the real business priorities, the specific challenges at hand. I'll point out hot topics and key stakeholders. In providing context for material, I may suggest ways to shape the delivery of the information. I have learned, however, to avoid rewriting the material. It is her expertise, not mine.

If possible, I'll proactively connect partner stars with key leaders or audience members ahead of time. Even a few phone calls or e-mail exchanges allow partner stars to learn more about audience interests directly and build credibility. With lone stars, I serve as a gatekeeper when possible to minimize unnecessary contact.

Third, let's talk about roles. What will the star take responsibility for doing, and what is my role? While A/V needs, material handouts and favorite beverages are usually discussed, I've found it as important to talk about how I can best prepare the audience for the day and to clarify the sustaining message needed.

After the Dance: What Remains?

The sustaining message is about what happens after the engagement. Some visits are simple exercises in exposure to new thinking with no expectation of follow-up. The better ones are leverage points to improve the organization.

It is a trap to spend all the preparation time on the event and skim over the day-after considerations. Lone stars may see the day after as simply timely payment for services rendered, or it might be booking a second act to reveal the most important information that was held back from the first visit. I usually stop at making sure the check is in the mail.

For the partner stars, the follow-up effort is usually degrees of stickiness. In the pre-meeting discussion, I try to clearly identify the single most important thing that must stick with participants after the presentation. Of course, the more meaningful the change, the more significant efforts and resources are needed, including the potential of a managed second engagement.

The first degree of stickiness concerns reinforcement. How can the key points of the event day be kept in the minds of the participants? Sending out short articles, how-to tools, notes of encouragement or Web-based reminders are all examples of ways to keep a topic alive.

The second degree of stickiness expands the notion of support with more extensive knowledge and skill transfer. This may translate into train-the-trainer or other ways of empowering internal staff. The third degree is about integration of the partner star's principles and tools into the HR system and practices. Rarely will this happen as a result of a speech, and it only occurs when the partner-star visit is part of a larger vision of change. Expecting one speech to do all the work is expecting too much.

So when the music starts playing and the dance is about to begin, it's best to figure out who is going to take you around the dance floor: a lone star or a partner star. Knowing which you have will help you take the right steps in planning and follow-up support.

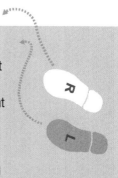

Next steps to consider:
- Where could you improve your learning and development efforts by finding great external partners?
- How can you identify the partner qualities most important to you and your organization early in the process of setting up an external consulting project?
- Is there a current consulting engagement that is not working out well that you should consider re-contracting for a better partnership?

PART THREE
EXECUTIVE DEVELOPMENT: STARS ON THE HORIZON

Executives — and executives in the making — make up a special part of the star universe. They are expected to transform from manager to leader, rally teams and organizations to superior performance, transition seamlessly to new and unknown circumstances and continue a lifelong development journey through it all. What's the right set of leadership expectations to guide progress? What role does the team play in developing a strong leader? What's needed is the right kind of support in their selection, movement and growth, when the dancing is smooth and also when it is challenging.

14. IS THIS LEADING SOMEWHERE?

Imagine trying to dance to music that is constantly changing, from ballroom to swing to breakdance and back again. This mash-up would keep everyone on his or her toes, but soon they would be out of step and looking for the exit. In a way, that's the state of leadership development today: ever-changing models, hot fads, heroic role models and short-lived to-do lists. We need a consistent playbook, well-executed, with the flexibility to engage different personal styles in order to help emerging stars grow to shining executives.

Does the world really need 38,542 different versions of leadership? That's a recent count of books offered on Amazon. Behind each book there is an author, a consultant and a different point of view on leadership. While it may be a confusing marketplace of ideas, leadership lies at the heart of talent management efforts. What do we think about our leaders today? Do we have enough leaders for tomorrow? How do we develop leaders?

What's the right version of leadership by the book to help us in our role as talent management champions? Let's take a stroll through a sample of the offerings.

By History

First there is a bookshelf — some parts dusty — stuffed with leadership based on historical figures. Need to toughen up? Try *Machiavelli on Modern Leadership, Patton on Leadership* or *Leadership Secrets of Attila the Hun*. For another view, pick your presidential role model, such as *Lincoln on Leadership, George Washington on Leadership* or *Ulysses S. Grant Strategies for Leadership*. Other historical choices include *Churchill on Leadership, A Higher Standard of Leadership: Lessons from the Life of Gandhi* and *The Power of Four: Leadership Lessons of Crazy Horse*.

By Metaphor

Move over to the next aisle and you'll go from the concrete lessons of history to the imaginative world of leadership by metaphor. A quick scan of titles urges readers to imagine leadership as an engine, as jazz, at high altitude, clearly artful, a cycle, a rhythm and rhyme. But it does get a bit confusing. Is it *Leadership From the Inside Out* or *Outdoor Leadership*? In the musical genre, is it *Leadership and the Art of the Conductor* or *Ensemble Leadership*? How about titles of leadership as a bus, a rock or naturally organic?

By Choice

If you think metaphoric leadership titles confuse, try choosing between *Feminine Leadership* or *My Little Black Book of Leadership* (lessons from ex-girlfriends); *Bold Leadership* or *Servant Leadership; Vince Lombardi on Leadership* or *The Leadership Secrets of Santa Claus.*

Care for something more down to earth? How about *The Imperfect Leader, Leadership for Dummies* or *The Complete Idiot's Guide to Motivational Leadership?*

By the Numbers

How about we sum it all up by looking at the "numbers" bookshelf of leadership. How many leadership rules are there? Here's a countdown:

- *The 417 Rules of Awesomely Bold Leadership*
- *Leading Every Day: 124 Actions for Effective Leadership*
- *The 100 Greatest Leadership Principles of All Time*
- *75 Principles of Conscious Leadership*
- *The Leadership Skills Handbook: 50 Key Skills from 1,000 Leaders*
- *The 21 Irrefutable Laws of Leadership*
- *Lead Well and Prosper: 15 Successful Strategies for Becoming a Good Manager*
- *7 Steps to Leadership Excellence*
- *5 Leadership Essentials for Women*
- *4 E's of Leadership*
- *1 Style of Leadership*

Finally, perhaps the most honest of the bunch, a title sitting on a shelf by itself: *A Very Short, Fairly Interesting and Reasonably Cheap Book About Studying Leadership.*

A Personal, Practical Playbook

Having read many of these books, heard from the authors or sat through their seminars, I find some of it useful, some nonsense and some quite confusing. For example if "the leadership secrets of X" are so unknown, why is it one of the most frequent titles? It can't be much of a secret.

Yet, tomorrow there will be more leadership titles on Amazon, new celebrity leaders to emulate and fresh metaphors for us to consider. It is certainly entertaining and speaks to a few deeper messages about the craft of developing star leaders.

First, leadership is a challenging and complex field of study. To be useful, it needs to connect personally. The manufacturing supervisor may better identify with a historical figure, while the marketing manager is inspired by a creative metaphor. The finance leader just wants a list to follow. In other words, what inspires and what instructs counts. We should allow for that variation.

Second, leadership needs to be practical. While allowing for freshness and inspiration, we should avoid chasing the fad of the moment. More leadership development efforts are wasted by spinning through the latest and loudest leadership fashions. The better books on leadership have much in common, a foundation that has been proven over time and not discovered last week.

Stick to the basics. All in all, the most useful and universal expectations have five simple components: trust, direction, innovation, people and results. Simple works better than complex. Remember, leaders throughout your organization — with different abilities and backgrounds — will have to master the same leadership dance moves.

Third, leadership needs to come from your playbook. Outside theories and stories are fine, but the real power is to set in place your organization's view of effective leadership. Your words, your history, your lessons well-executed over time will grow the best leaders.

Next steps:

- Can you identify the predominant model of leadership expectations in your organization? How well-known and consistent is it?

- Are these expectations robust enough to stand up to changing circumstances and strategic shifts? If not, how can you build more durability into the model to account for changes?

- Do your current and upcoming talent development efforts clearly communicate and reinforce one common playbook of leadership?

Your next move:

On-board a new leader, and get the team on-board with the new leader.

15. GETTING THE TEAM ON-BOARD

First moves set the tone for the rest of the performance. On the dance floor, both partners need to be set and in sync before the first steps are taken. The first steps in the partnership between a new executive and a team are also critical. Preparing the team to be led is as important as instructing the new leader on how to begin.

An often-overlooked aspect of assimilating a new external executive into a company is not getting that person on-board with the organization but vice versa. When the new executive takes the reins of leadership, the question then becomes whether the team is ready to be led.

Every seasoned manager comes into a new business with a sense of excitement and anxiety. There's excitement about the opportunities promised during the interview process and anxiety in discovering the unknowns. A newcomer might experience a love-hate relationship with the new team and peers: The organization loves the fresh perspective, new ideas and new practices but hates that the new person just won't leave things alone. The new leader wants to lead change.

There are two events that can accelerate a productive working relationship with a new leader — one early on in the on-boarding process and a second about six months later.

Early Assimilation Team Session

One of the best tools to overcome resistance to new leaders is a set of assimilation questions. Although deceptively simple on the surface, these questions can help a new leader and the organization in profound ways. They are based on the notion that meaningful relationship building and an open exchange serve as a solid platform for leadership.

I've used four primary questions with leaders and their teams about two to three months into the new job. At that point, both parties have covered the basics, and it's time to get down to the leader's moment of truth.

1. **What does the team know about the leader?** What does the team want to know? Some new leaders are better than others at self-disclosure. Few are good at mind reading. Teams are more willing to trust and follow leaders when potentially sensitive topics are covered early, and in a direct way. These probes can reveal useful areas for understanding, such as:

- **Background and career:** What were the leader's most developmental jobs? Who were the most influential bosses? How long does the leader plan on staying in the role? What's next?

> **There is no greater time for learning than when a new leader joins an organization — and no greater opportunity for misunderstanding and missteps.**

- **Communication style and preferences:** In person, e-mail or voice mail? Scheduled or drop-in meetings? Headlines or detailed messages?

- **Likes and dislikes:** Everyone has pet peeves and preferences. Must meetings start and end exactly on time, or is a bit late OK? Should problems be reported early or only after potential solutions can be offered?

- **Expectations and direction:** What results are most important to achieve? Short term? Longer term? How do other senior managers view the team, the situation and what needs to change?

2. **What does the leader need to know about the team, and how does it like to be led?** Now, the focus shifts from the manager to the team. Getting team members to talk about themselves facilitates group bonding with the new leader. Discussing how team members prefer to be led allows them to describe many of the topics the leader shared in the previous two questions, such as communication styles and preferences.

3. **What challenges might the leader face?** Part of getting a team on-board with a new leader is having the group put itself in the place of the

leader. This topic builds empathy and a bridge to the new leader. Groups often link challenges with what the leader has shared about goals and expectations.

4. **What are the team's challenges and potential solutions?** The challenges the team shares can provide the leader with an inside view of the team's thinking, including how the team views its situation in the organization, their pressures and creative approaches to consider. When I see a leader and a team connecting well, they often remark, "We have the same challenges." This can be an encouraging sign of maturity in the group. It is certainly a sign the team is getting on-board with the new leader. That's the moment of truth awaiting all new leaders.

Six-Month Reconnect

The on-boarding journey of a new leader and team continues for some time. While the early assimilation meeting helps, there is a need for a reconnect session at about the six-month mark. At this stage, everyone moves on from early hope and anxiety to confirmed optimism and possible concern. Blind spots can develop by this stage, but there is still time for a mid-course correction.

After reminding the leader and team of the six-month reconnect session, send out a simple survey to the team members. The purpose of the survey is to allow team members to give their current impression on how the leader and team are doing. The survey items consist of factors most important at this stage. Usually a subset of a standard leadership survey, a sample of the items would include:

• The right amount of clear direction and priority setting.

• The appropriate amount of challenge and risk taking in change efforts.

• Leader is listening well and responding to input.

• Understanding and appropriate respect for the culture.

• Establishing working relationships with key stakeholders.

• Demonstrating flexibility in approaches and processes.

• Delivering the right amount of early wins and results while building for long-term success.

Of course, items can be added to the survey that incorporate hot spots in your organization that trip up leaders and teams early. The scale for the survey is a relative one, with choices such as "better than expected," "on track," "needing some improvement," "needing significant improvement." The survey ends with three open-ended questions: What are two to three things the leader is doing well and should continue? What two to three things should the leader do now to improve or sustain success? What two to three things do the team members need to do now for leader and team success? The leader can take the survey as well for a self-assessment to compare to the team results.

Once the survey results are collected, an HR leader or consultant can walk the leader through the findings and help craft a communication and action plan. Next, the team should process the survey results together and prepare for the reconnect meeting when the leader and team discuss the findings, explore important areas for progress and agree on follow-up steps. As with early assimilation, having a trusted HR leader or consultant facilitate the meeting helps keep the atmosphere positive and open.

Early Investments Pay Off

There is no greater time for learning than when a new leader joins an organization — and no greater opportunity for misunderstanding and missteps. Assimilation isn't just about getting the new leader informed and integrated. It's also about readying the organization so the new manager can lead. Taking two steps in the first six months of the new leader-team relationship is a smart investment that pays off with accelerated working relationships and performance.

Next steps:

- What practices do you have in place to help a new leader and team get off to a good start?

- Are there key new leader-team situations in which more investments should be made in the on-boarding process?

- At the six-month mark, do you have productive reconnect practices, such as the team survey, to keep a positive on-boarding process going?

Your next move:

Get your leadership stars to share their lessons with others.

16. STARS IN THEIR COURSES

Senior leaders are increasingly asked to play a more active role in the education of emerging executives. Being guided by someone who has taken all the right career steps — or learned well the lessons of a few missteps — is a promising approach. But it needs to be tailored to the setting, as well as the natural abilities of the leader-teacher.

While never done here before, the excited CEO thought it was a good idea. His savvy senior management team played along. And when I got the call to help out, I knew it was going to be quite a learning experience.

The notion? Replace the faculty of our proven executive development courses with our own senior officers. This was during my days at GE Crotonville, long before leaders teaching leaders became popular. Then, CEO Jack Welch was convinced that early internal efforts by Pepsi and others proved a superior way of grooming future stars.

The benefits? For students, they were credible lessons learned from successful leaders inside the organization and a rare chance to interact with a senior leader in a mostly open forum to exchange ideas and hear entertaining stories from the life of an executive.

For executives, it was the opportunity to deliver a message and lesson they passionately believe matters for the organization and the future executives. It was also a chance to hear directly from an important talent layer whose feedback under normal circumstances would be filtered through the chain of command. Furthermore, the teaching executive was also learning: about different ways of influencing and about the practical application of the subject matter.

To the talent management leader, it was a chance to transform an executive development course into a dynamic forum in which all the potential benefits for students and executives would be realized. To make it all happen, I first had to learn about tailoring.

A Question of Fit

In the month leading up to the first program, I spent a good deal of time helping the half-dozen senior executives designated by the CEO to be the inaugural faculty. I quickly realized that some saw the benefits early and enthusiastically dove into the task of preparing their material and method for the course. Others proved more challenging. Their schedules were demanding and their interest in the new classroom assignment was questionable.

> **The big lesson of internal executive teachers is that it takes a star to make a star.**

One executive stands out in particular. After rejecting the standard offerings I gave him, in desperation I asked him to consider teaching something that was sitting on his desk. "Surely there is an interesting story or case study somewhere in the inbox or stack of reports that would fit nicely with the financial section of the course," I said. Lucky for me and the next class, he was in a forgiving mood and did find a recently closed acquisition that was prime material and soon became a highly rated session.

The lessons I learned helping the first six executives become valued teachers have been repeated in the years that followed as leaders teaching leaders became a proven development method. The most important lesson was to manage the fit between the purpose of the course, the assets and the executive's preferences. As program leader, I had to move beyond the initial instinct to please the executive and hold true to the objectives of the course. Executives had to align their message to the program learning goals and not hijack the class for their own purposes — although that still happened occasionally.

A Sample of Six Choices for Leaders Teaching

I had to stay attuned to the abilities and comfort level of each executive. Some were natural teachers, Socratic facilitators and wonderful storytellers. Others were good businesspeople but not teachers. Over time, we expanded the definition of leaders to teaching leaders wider. A range of different choices emerged that I still use today to entice line leaders into the classroom:

• Joe brought the full-steam-ahead style into the classroom by presenting a passionate and straightforward presentation and engaged the audience with his excitement and expectation that the stars in the audience would reciprocate with their reactions and ideas.

- Steve, on the other hand, humbly taught by example, sharing highlights and lowlights from his own 360 and quite transparently revealed what he was trying to improve.

- Paula had a fully thought-out theory of her work and used the class as an opportunity to air out her ideas, encouraging others to help her prove her thinking.

- Ben taught by question, raising an intriguing and ambiguous situation and respectfully playing the differing student opinions off each other as a way of deepening executive thinking skills.

- Chris enjoyed throwing a topic into breakout groups and then molding the recommendations to balance risk-taking innovation and practical execution reality.

- Eunice was not really at her best in front of the classroom but masterful as a coach, helping teams navigate through a business simulation.

Teachable Moments

Today, it's not uncommon to find an executive teaching an organization's training curriculum. The traditional formal classroom setting has evolved into more informal situations in which a line leader will take advantage of a teachable moment in the normal course of business and provide valuable lessons learned. All in all, the big lesson is it takes a star to make a star.

Next steps:

- Are there formal courses in which internal teaching faculty would be more effective?

- How can you best define the fit necessary to match the purpose of the course and the gifts and preferences of the line executive asked to teach?

- Are there informal ways you can extend leaders teaching leaders to everyday settings in your organization?

Your next move:

There is still a valuable role for external teachers, but don't abandon internal support.

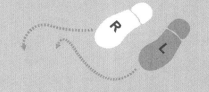

17. INSIDE AN OUTSIDE COACHING JOB

Executive coaching is a common and potentially effective resource to keep a star's development on track. Internal HR staff or talent management leaders often are not part of the coaching engagement, causing the investment to be less than optimal. There are specific ways internal support can play a key role at the start, middle and end of a coaching engagement to ensure success.

When the executive coach steps in, do you step out? One of the most popular trends in development inside an organization is reaching outside for a coach's services. In many cases, there is great value in tapping into the sea of consultants. But removing yourself from the situation once the coach arrives can be a mistake.

There are three areas in which an internal development professional can make a difference in the success or failure of an external coaching arrangement.

Managing the Coaching Checklist

Every coaching engagement has milestones and critical events. Having a checklist is a useful way to plot productive engagements. Here's a sample:

- **Start-up steps:** Does this coaching engagement make sense? Have I established agreed-upon expectations with the key stakeholders? Are we clear on what we are trying to improve? How are we going to measure results? Is coaching the right solution, or should this be handled by the employee's manager? Early on, coaching objectives are often fluid, so insiders must remain in the conversation. The result is a triangular contract between the coach, leader and internal development professional.

- **Middle steps:** Have I set a schedule of periodic check-ins with both the leader and the coach to gauge progress? Ask the leader how coaching is going and what has been achieved. How much follow-up is the leader doing with his or her manager? Ask the coach if the leader is making progress and how responsive the leader is to coaching.

An insider might hesitate to keep tabs on the coaching progress because of a concern about confidentiality. There is a need for conversations outside the normal boundaries of an organization, but in the end, coaching is a business investment made to improve leadership capabilities.

- **Next steps:** How will I manage the process of closure and evaluate success? What will be the standards and methods to assess progress? How will we bring closure to the project? What follow-up support and further check-ins might we consider?

Whatever the agreed-upon option, you should have a three-way conversation to review results and determine next steps. A leader's development is an ongoing journey, and an external coaching intervention is one step along the way. Determining what comes next continues the development.

Manage the Relationship

Company insiders need to navigate the agendas of the leader, coach, boss and other key stakeholders. It's helpful to have a working relationship with each coach in the external pool. Often, this is a partnership to broker the right coach for the leader, keep in touch and remove obstacles to coaching impact.

As assignments with the external coach conclude, it's time to step in to maintain progress. At the very least, map out next steps and resources after the coach departs. Occasionally, it means doing more. Following up doesn't take long, and it keeps leaders focused on the right behavior as they implement new leadership practices.

As stewards of company resources, our inside role is to jump in on the front end of an engagement, provide discipline in managing the process and ensure solid follow-up support when the external coach leaves. These efforts are important as leaders navigate the demands of the role and avoid a common problem in executive life: the derailment bullet that can't be dodged.

Next steps:

- Do you have a well-coordinated process for identifying and managing executive coaching assignments?
- Are there opportunities in the beginning of the coaching engagement to ensure expectations are set well and lead to productive outcomes?
- Can you provide mid-engagement check-ins and closure support to improve current and future coaching investments?

Your next move:

Use four resources to help developing stars avoid burning out.

18. RESOURCES TO AVOID THE BULLET

Most missteps on the dance floor can be quickly corrected and the dance will continue with little lasting negative impact. However, there is an all-too-common phenomenon in executive life in which even the most talented stars meet a challenge that trips them up. Called derailment, it needs to be recognized and addressed as part of any vibrant talent management practice.

Winston Churchill once said, "Nothing in life is so exhilarating as to be shot at without results." In other words, the bullet missed and I am now paying full attention. I would add that nothing provides better focus for serious personal development than witnessing a career-ending bullet shot at someone else.

You've likely been a witness to career derailment, that curious phenomenon in which talented, driven leaders end up out the door rather than moving up the ranks.

In addition to working to help my company's executives build immunity to derailment, I often have the chance to present the concept to MBA students. These ambitious, hard-driving future stars are often surprised to understand that smarts, superior technical skills and self-motivation alone don't guarantee they can avoid career disappointment.

The presentation begins by deconstructing cases of successful stars that suddenly flame out. The surface derailment factors are, unsurprisingly, failure to achieve expected results or, surprising to some, achieving results in a destructive way. There are usually one to five factors underlying these headlines:

- Lacked strategic thinking and retained too much tactical work.
- Had all the strategic thinking needed but couldn't execute well.
- Didn't influence and build relationships effectively across the matrix organization.
- Failed to build and motivate a strong team.
- Demonstrated an unrecoverable crack in personal integrity and character.

These factors surface most during times of change. In other words, the leader was doing fine and then experienced a transition, such as a new job, new boss or new circumstances, which made these dormant weaknesses critical job factors.

The Transition Challenge

At this point, most MBA students are interested and push to understand how to avoid it in the first place. My response is to draw two charts about navigating transitions. At the onset of a career, technical skills matter more than managerial or strategic leadership. Becoming an executive shifts the order of importance.

The first chart reminds us that moving from manager to executive requires new skills. Most new executives think they have arrived and no longer need to keep up a rigorous personal learning agenda. Further, they often become deaf to negative feedback. If that happens, sooner or later the derailment bullets start flying.

To continue learning as an executive, I drew a simple chart of resources vs. demands. As transitions occur, professional and personal demands increase. One must continually build new resources to keep up with new demand.

> **As transitions occur, professional and personal demands increase. One must continually build new resources to keep up with new demands.**

Four Ways for Executives to Build Resources

I have seen successful executives add resources in four main areas: hands, heart, head and whole.

"Hands" means physical health. Strong leaders meet new demands well if they have a good physical base, especially exercise, eating and sleeping. Cutting corners here to meet our 24/7, always-on world will mean less endurance and energy to draw upon. Recent brain research reminds us that exercise builds brainpower.

"Heart" means emotions and relationships. Leaders often underestimate the impact their emotional demeanor has on others throughout the organization. Leaders under stress facing unexpected personal or professional demands need to draw upon their emotional intelligence to manage their emotions, as well as authentically connect with others. Maintaining affirming and renewing relationships is key. As with exercise, cutting back on time and personal engagement with important relationships can undermine a leader's effectiveness.

"Head" means the practices that build perspective. Derailing leaders often spend too much time on the runway of their work and don't gain appropriate altitude to see the bigger picture. It's a critical instinct to know when to jump from a daily tactical, project-oriented focus to a more strategic, vision-oriented view. Having routines and reminders can help. Getting coaching and tools to be effective at each level also is critical.

"Whole" means always being grounded in purpose. The ultimate source of energy to grow and meet new demands is a heartfelt commitment to a personal calling or reason for being. Great leaders continually remind themselves why they go about their work. I shared with the class my centering purpose is to connect people with their full potential.

The Organization Checklist

The organization plays a role, in concert with budding stars, to build strong resources to navigate transitions and derailment challenges. Based on internal and external post-mortems of executive derailment, this checklist can be useful to help the organization:

When considering a promotion:

- Are we confident this selection isn't too much of a stretch?
- Does the leader lack the required new skills and experiences, especially for the job requirements?
- Are we confusing performance with potential (and readiness)?

When issues surface:

- Are we ignoring this problem and hoping it will get better on its own? (It rarely does.)
- Are we devoting adequate time and resources to support the new leader, especially in difficult roles with frequent turnover?

For ongoing talent development:

- Have we provided the tools and development to prepare the leader for the next job?
- Are we selecting and coaching for resiliency and adaptability?
- Are we building confidence and self-insight and humility into our talent?

• Are we adequately communicating and reinforcing our values and integrity standard?

Failure is uncomfortable and usually avoided in training and communication. We need to provide the right balance, building for success and also teaching and acting in ways that avoid the bullets of derailment. In addition to good checklists and development resources, numerous tools can give leaders information on how they are impacting others and keep them on track, including 360 surveys.

Next steps:

• Have you identified the most common derailment factors of your executives?

• Are derailment and leadership shortcomings an open topic in your talent management practice, and can you incorporate checklists to better manage leadership problems?

• How can you help developing leaders build resources to make it through challenging transitions?

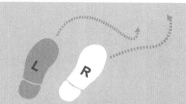

Your next move:

360 surveys are the most commonly used — and overused — tool in the industry. Some leaders are inundated with surveys and wish for their last 360.

19. THE LAST 360

Too much of a good thing? It seems to happen with most talent management practices. We start with early success and are encouraged to widely apply new tools. But not every bright idea works well for everyone in every circumstance. Talent development leaders need perspective and discipline in applying a portfolio of tools to best help stars develop.

Scene One: A hotel bar after a daylong business meeting with a near-retirement executive.

"You caught me," he said. "I thought I had my last 360 and then you launched that new leadership program with the feedback survey last month. Now I guess I have to go through one more."

Scene Two: A coffee shop near the office with a mid-career executive.

"That feedback wasn't half bad," she said. "I picked up a few pointers. I hope my team feels the same when they go through it."

Scene Three: At my desk the next day, reflecting how differently these two leaders reacted to the same thing.

It was too easy to dismiss the feedback-averse old-timer as developmentally arrested and retired on the job. I've bumped into leaders with similar attitudes in nearly all age groups and levels.

Yet, the coffee shop conversation reminded me of the value of helping leaders stay on track with perspective-building information. Research points out that many leaders develop a blind spot on how they are coming across to their team and peers as they move up. That gap in insight is a leading cause of talent derailment. Even mature leaders can be re-energized and reminded they can serve as mentors. So it might be worth taking the heat and subjecting our talent to these surveys.

So Cool Back in the Day

I remember when 360s were the hot new management tool. The technique of gathering feedback on a leader from peers, subordinates and bosses had escaped the confines of selected training programs, such as the Benchmark 360 in CCL classes, and was rapidly spreading across the land.

CEOs publicly proclaimed its virtues, and whole conferences were devoted to its nuances. Soon, consulting firms of all shapes and sizes discovered a new billable service and launched an arms race for more sophisticated feedback models, flashy online sites and somewhat questionable proprietary research. Studies pointed out that firms using 360s created more shareholder value. Eventually, internal training managers figured out they could apply it to all manner of talent management challenges.

> **Research points out that many leaders develop a blind spot on how they are coming across to their employees as they move up in the organization.**

New manager training? Give them a 360. Performance appraisal? Let 360 scores determine rating and pay. An executive needs a bit of coaching? Throw in a 360. Everyone wants self-service? Offer on-demand 360. How's our 360 program doing? Let's get some survey feedback. Overdone? Not quite yet. Mom or dad executive not doing so well with the home team? Let's gather 360 from family members.

Then the consultants produced cutting-edge research showing that firms using 360s produce less shareholder value. The whole journey of the 360 followed the typical overdone arc of talent management innovation and abuse, from concept to commercial to comical. No wonder managers are counting backward from retirement to determine their last 360 indignity.

Is the 360 Worth Saving?

More or less: less assuming everything is a feedback opportunity, and more finding the right time to offer a 360, such as transition points and job changes.

We need less of slamming 360s into annual appraisals and using mathematical calculations to judge performance. Repeated studies show 360s become less effective in appraisals, as rating becomes too political and raters play it safe, providing non-offensive ratings and bland comments.

We need more managers gathering informal opinions from key stakeholders as input to an appraisal and then forming their own judgment of performance.

We need more providing a balance in the message. Only about a third of leaders need to focus on the negative or "developmental opportunities" found in a report. Most of us obsess about any feedback as threatening criticism. While some would benefit by addressing the low scores and comments in a report, most would benefit by looking for good, relevant behaviors to strengthen. Good 360 practices reinforce that approach and provide useful tools and support to easily translate strength building to practical actions.

360s need less complexity and redundancy. They have grown to well over 100 items and 50-plus page reports to digest. That's too much information, and getting the same feedback annually leads to feedback fatigue.

We need more short surveys with the most relevant items and brief feedback reports that highlight key messages in action-oriented formats.

We need more of rejuvenating the method and content from time to time. I've recently been combining a shorter 360 with a valid personality instrument for my leaders.

As with much talent development practice, fresh new ideas can be overused and grow stale. 360 feedback has gone that route. We need to bring it back into balance as one of many good ways to help stars develop.

Next steps:

- Are there tools and practices you overuse in situations where other solutions may work better?

- Do you have the right balance of self-insight tools such as 360s in your talent management practice?

- Are improvements needed in your 360 practice to make it better serve your leaders today?

PART FOUR
HR EXCELLENCE: GETTING THE BAND TOGETHER

Talent management is not a single department's job in leading-edge HR organizations; it is the primary mission of the whole function.

Much like musicians in a band, everyone in HR has a part to play in the performance. Knowing the business well, being influential and earning trust are key for each individual making a contribution. But the magic happens when every individual note blends into a special rhythm and harmony.

There are quite a few ways to keep the HR members playing the same music. Integration happens at the team level, as well as with new, comprehensive information systems. It happens by finding ways to standardize together and keep programs and services fresh by knowing what to initiate and what to retire together.

Having a track record of team success garners CEO-level support to keep the music playing and the talent stars shining bright.

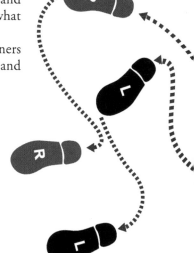

20. HR: DO YOU GET IT?

No one wants to be off-key while playing music together, and likewise, no one in HR strives to be out of sync when playing a tune together. Yet, we can drift and need to constantly check for alignment and what really matters in our daily performance, from business partners to enterprise leaders.

The rant began before the second glass of wine was served. I was dining with two marketing executives recently when the pair started venting their frustrations about how HR was missing the point. One of them paused midway through the venting, and said, "Now Kevin, understand that we like you and you get it; our issues are with those HR types that don't get it."

I think that was a compliment, but I didn't feel great about the tone of the discussion. Like it or not, I've observed business executives dividing the HR community into two classifications: those who get it and those who miss the point. Those who get it find themselves in highly sought-after business partnerships. Those labeled otherwise are on the outside looking in.

Reflecting on that dinner encounter and considering the most influential HR leaders I've known over the years — as well as some of my HR friends who spent most of their time on the outside looking in — I've come to a few conclusions.

First, getting it is fundamental to being a strong HR contributor. Second, in describing someone as getting it, a leader is describing someone who has a firm grasp on the business, appreciates the line leader's agenda and views the work of HR as secondary.

Here are my three big skills for getting it:

1. **Business first:** My role is to contribute to the business first and serve my HR role second. "Win, have fun and make a buck," was the slogan of one of my mentors at GE years ago. His quote still resonates as a reminder that my job is to help the team win customers, not produce shiny

new HR initiatives for their own sake. I've always been curious about the business as much as the development profession. I am a constant student of investor reports, internal financial reports and business plans. Moreover, I try to start every conversation with line leaders by discussing their business, what's new, how the new product is working and how the numbers are this quarter. Business first, then we can move on to the HR agenda.

2. **Working the map:** In my early days at General Mills, I didn't have a feel for the business or how to navigate the organization. These were challenges to overcome if I was going to matter to the organization. In addition to reading every report I could get my hands on and buying coffee for every available finance and marketing manager I could befriend, I also began studying those who were most successful at creating change in the organization. What impressed me most was their knowledge of where to build coalitions and influence key stakeholders. They seemed to possess an unofficial, invisible organizational chart that guided their actions. Relationship building is a key skill and a constant focus of my time, and it's never-ending work.

> **Like it or not, business executives divide HR into those who get it and those who miss the point.**

In addition to the map, these high influencers introduced me to the concept of executive presence. When the path to change placed them in front of senior executives, they had a crisp, confident and relaxed style. As I grew in the job, I found it easier to at least fake being confident and relaxed. The crisp part took some time. I had to temper my enthusiasm to explain everything I knew about a topic when given the chance. Even today, I have to be reminded to give the headline first and cut my comments short when body language signals they've heard what they need.

3. **Good judgment:** HR stars are trusted advisers with something valuable to contribute to a group conversation or a coaching encounter.

One of my favorite stories is about the new apprentice who asked his mentor how to acquire good judgment. "From experience!" replied the mentor. When the apprentice asked how to acquire the necessary experience, the mentor wisely concluded, "From poor judgment!" While poor judgment is a recipe for career derailment rather than success, the scar tissue developed from hard-fought battles is part of the professional journey.

Learn from the battle experiences of others to build better judgment, too. Seek out top performers and wise counselors to share what they've learned. That way you can accelerate your judgment capabilities and solidify an impressive support network. Whether it's from your own experience or others, step back and reflect on what's going on and what can be learned. It is all too easy to fall into the eager-to-serve trap and not take time to reflect. A friend of mine calls it "getting up to the balcony and away from the dance floor." Observe the situation and rise above the noise and distractions of the moment. It's about gaining perspective that ultimately builds great judgment.

Like it or not, many leaders divide HR into two camps: those who get it and those who don't. The former is a much more rewarding and fun place to be, but it needs to be earned over and over again. Make investments in your business acumen, organizational influence and judgment.

Next steps:

- How would others rate your reputation in the organization today? How can increasing your business acumen in the organization benefit you and your talent development work?
- How can you communicate "business first, then the HR agenda" when working with your business leaders?
- In what ways can you invest in developing sharper judgment in your work, reach out to your network to learn more and make time to gain perspective?

Your next move:

Individual efforts to get it matter, but coordinate HR efforts to have a profound impact.

21. ALL TOGETHER IN THE BAND

One dance move can make a good impression, but when all the moves of a routine are choreographed, the end result is impressive. Today, the individual parts of talent management are being put together to integrate the total body of work. New software systems are often the driver of integration but having a unified system and playing well together are two different things. The choreography of talent management integration is the effort to bring the musicians together as one band rather than just rewriting the musical scores.

"Integrated talent management" is one of the top buzz phrases in our industry right now. The idea is that aligning the various disciplines and data streams of talent work can create higher value and more impact.

In theory, it's a great idea. In practice, the reality of knitting things together is hard work with frustrating barriers. Fortunately, there are enablers of collaborative teamwork.

People and Systems

Classic organizational design principles call for work to be broken down into subunits for appropriate focus and to optimize the resources of a specialty. It usually works quite well. The people in compensation create programs to deliver cost-effective and competitive pay practices. The recruiters bring in the most qualified new employees as quickly as possible. The pros in learning and development crank out online and classroom material for those well-paid, well-placed employees. These HR specialties set their strategies and objectives in isolation from each other. The cycle of new practices and change initiatives spring forth mostly independently. Rewards and resources go to the subsets, rarely the whole team.

HR's information age ushered in automation to more efficiently manage the transactions of each subgroup. Compensation systems process payroll and incentives. Recruiting systems sort resumes and track candidates.

Learning management systems document competencies and class completions. Each is state of the art from a different software vendor. Over time, the attempts to link systems and the best system providers are promoting integrated suites of talent management systems. The evolution is promising, but the conversion process usually means someone sacrifices his or her favorite functionality for the greater good.

How Together?

There are barriers aplenty to integration, but there is hope as well. It takes extra effort and the kind of intelligent, willful change management effort we advise our business partners to apply. A few common enablers can pull the practices and systems of talent management together:

> **Talent management integration takes extra effort and the kind of intelligent and willful change management efforts that we advise clients to apply.**

- **Common planning:** Author and consultant Patrick Lencioni presents a thematic goal as a way to pull multiple departments together. You can craft a talent management thematic goal by posing the question, "If we don't get anything else done in the next six months together, we must do ... ?" Getting specific multiple-unit efforts behind the common thematic creates a road map to achieve the collective mission. When the short-term thematic goal is reached, the planning cycle is repeated and the success builds momentum for future teamwork.

- **Clear accountability and measures:** Integration means great teamwork. As in the sports world, winning teams perform because of clearly understood and coordinated individual contributions. It is all too common to see promising HR initiatives unwind due to the simple lack of dedicated time to establish and revisit role expectations. Once established, an integrated talent management thematic should be followed by asking and answering the questions, "Who is going to do what by when to make this happen?" as well as "How will we monitor and measure progress?"

- **Competent processes:** Smart, integrated talent management software installations map out the current and optimal processes and then configure the system to effectively enable the complete practice, not just those in any one subunit. Getting different HR departments together to create a mutual view of how real work happens is always educational and sometimes transformational. But don't let the software impose practices that are too aggressive. I've never seen an organization overcome poor talent management habits by imposing a sophisticated out-of-the-box software package.

- **Collaborative values:** Let's be candid here. There can be peer jealousies and functional infighting across HR departments. Integrating the hardware of talent management calls for an investment in the software of mutual trust and collaboration. Devoting time to bring different groups together to renew healthy relationships is as smart an investment as any new software package.

Integration makes sense, but recognize the hard work that goes into overcoming entrenched obstacles, past habits and legacy systems when launching an integration initiative. Ensure high-performing teams are in place with aligned goals, clear roles, effective processes and healthy relationships. Keep in mind that healthy relationships need to navigate the natural differences in style and preferences that may hold us apart.

Next steps:

- How would you assess the current state of integration across the HR function? What are the best opportunities to work in common for greater collective impact?

- How can you leverage new software and programming to blend the work of talent management across functional departments?

- How can you inspire greater levels of teamwork through common planning, shared

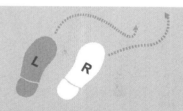

metrics, competent processes and collaborative relationship building?

Your next move:

Help your team find a way to work with "those people."

22. DANCING WITH 'THOSE PEOPLE'

For some, picking up a new dance routine is easy. For others, getting both the left and right foot to move in the right direction is a challenge. At times, each foot has a mind of its own and doesn't seem connected to the rest of the body. HR and other organizational teams often feel the same way. While connected in a meaningful way, each acts independently, making for a disjointed performance. High-quality learning and development initiatives can promote common understanding, better teamwork and get the disparate parts moving in the same direction.

Is there anything more challenging than pulling a cohesive team together from different parts of the organization? While some team-building and metrics alignment work can help, I've observed something deeper going on.

A core career belief influences how most people act in an organization and this creates quite a barrier. Most manufacturing and operations professionals believe that anything can be repeated with the right process. Their point of view is, "See that pen? I can make another one just like it if we identify and follow the right process!"

Marketing and sales types are grounded in the belief we can make a deal. Every situation is unique, and there is value to be created if we just can get together and agree.

Technical people — engineers, scientists or even finance and legal folks — see the world as a problem to be solved. Frame the problem right, plug in the right input and a logical solution can be found. The world can be ordered; we just need logic. The collective view of human resources leaders? Their core belief is, "We can help."

When leaders of different beliefs get together, sometimes things work, and sometimes it is chaos. We often organize learning events that reinforce the silos rather than break down these barriers. It's more comfortable and natural to stick with one's own and complain about "those other people" who get in the way, because birds of a feather learn together and reinforce common beliefs and biases. If they would only learn more about each other, and even learn together, the whole company might work better.

Three Ways to Mix It Up

Training can break down internal barriers in a number of ways. The nature of education often can provide a more open atmosphere to explore differences and reach new levels of understanding. There are three primary ways to modify learning programs to build stronger cross-functional bridges:

- **Mixing groups:** Whenever possible, blend different groups together. A while back, I was faced with integrating two corporate cultures after a merger. I used a new leadership development program for the top 500 executives as a mixing intervention. Each class was a radical blend of career fields and company heritages. It worked great, and many leaders remarked that spending time together forged new relationships over the material and provided a common language for the new executive group.

> "One of the most significant contributions we can make to an organization is to remove barriers.

- **Mixing resources:** One way to break down boundaries is to broaden the resources used to provide learning. I've brought in speakers from different parts of the company to enrich a single-function learning event. Using a sales executive as faculty for an engineering course doubles the learning, as teacher and participant gain insight together. General orientation material from one function, such as a Marketing 101 e-learning module, could be integrated into a finance program.

- **Mixing the focus:** Action learning projects are popular and powerful learning tools because you can structure cross-boundary learning into the curriculum. A comprehensive business simulation is another great method for promoting cross-functional learning. One of my favorite simulations pulls leaders from all over the corporation into cross-functional teams to manage a start-up company. Each leader must play a functional role different from his or her current one. Leaders gain great insight into how someone else sees the world, as well how all functions contribute to the whole.

One of the most significant contributions we can make to an organization is to remove barriers. Every program and learning event can either reinforce existing boundaries or chip away at the walls inside an enterprise. Energy spent reinforcing the functional silos and mindsets wastes talent and time. Building bridges inside a company leverages internal talent to better serve external customers. It all starts with re-examining your role as bridge-builder in your organization.

Next steps:

- What are the organizational boundaries and barriers that cause resource and performance drains?

- Where could better understanding and collaboration across boundaries improve performance and bring the best out of your talent?

- What are the opportunities to launch or re-engineer training efforts to support cross-boundary understanding, relationship building and teamwork?

Your next move:

Strike the right balance between customization and standardization in talent management routines.

23. CUSTOMIZE OR STANDARDIZE

Star dancers have their signature moves that shine through when they perform. Look closely and you'll see that customization is built upon a solid foundation of standard practice and discipline. In other words, they master the basics first and then add special value by tailoring and adapting when needed. In the same way, the best performing organizations have discipline and established standards and customize only when it is truly a value-added signature.

Three times in my career, I've built a case for standardization while launching a refreshed performance management system. Each time, the clincher has been showcasing a thick stack of performance appraisal templates choking the company. It's hard to believe such a muddled collection of formats, competencies and measurement weightings comes from one company. What began years ago as a simple talent management practice had morphed into a confusing mess of unnecessary complexity and questionable quality.

In short, well-meaning HR generalists and line leaders felt compelled to change something that would have served them well as it was originally designed.

The case for standardization in talent management is quite evident. It offers efficiency and scale, providing common practices and language to align the organization. Providing useful tools to busy HR generalists can simplify their work, instead of having them reinvent the wheel for every local need.

Centers of excellence can collect the best practices or apply the best thinking. This approach avoids the questionable belief some HR leaders have that the way to gain respect is to create everything from scratch, with heavy involvement from business line leaders. There is a science to great HR, and we diminish our professional standing by over-customization. Do responsible finance professionals let line leaders create their own accounting standards? The application of a standard process eliminates waste and maximizes effectiveness.

All Meaning Is Local

HR has much to gain by skillfully standardizing talent management practice. Of course, allowance should be made for occasional variation. There are times when a standard practice doesn't resonate with parts of an organization and requires a process to connect employees with the topic at hand. Some tailoring to adapt and create local meaning can be justified. Just be sure it's the exception and not the rule.

One other benefit from some customization is that new ideas can be piloted in parts of the organization and, if successful, standardized throughout the enterprise. Good talent management ideas are not exclusively generated from the executive suite or HR centers of excellence. Champion standardization where scale, efficiency and effectiveness offer the greatest value to the enterprise. But allow some flexibility, too.

> **I've learned to champion standardization on what matters most, where scale, efficiency and effectiveness offer the greatest value.**

Three Principles to Standardize Together

Respect the need to create on a local level and leave them alone when it makes sense. Allowing customization provides multiple experiments and is a source of innovation. The next great idea in talent management can come from these experiments and be scaled throughout the organization. Try these three key principles to standardize work while respecting local needs:

- **Be sensitive to local needs when creating the "perfect" enterprise solution to a talent management practice.** Involve key users early in the design process to get a handle on what is needed and what adjustments will be needed.

- **Build in options for customization.** The need for HR generalists to show value is legitimate. They need to be seen as strategic and creative, not just mindless administrators of corporate missives. Designate certain core practices or tools as unalterable and also provide space for local questions on an employee opinion survey or alternatives in the form of appraisal rating factors.

- **Ensure adequate communication and training support.** There is a wrong-headed belief that centers of excellence add the most value by creating the perfect tool or practice. Hitting the send button announcing the new practice alone is inadequate. Value is added at the point of execution, not in the back office. Half of the time and resources to any new practice, such as a new leadership model or assessment tool, should be devoted to communication and capability training as the program is launched.

Unless there is guidance, everything will be customized, often without adding much value. Of course, there is a benefit to adapting and innovating – where there is clear reason. The best talent management organizations create useful standards and routines that work for the majority of circumstances, with the right amount of upfront involvement of end users to ensure effectiveness. But within a standard, design options to allow some localization, with proper investments in communication and training to help those using the final product. Over time, well-implemented standards are both efficient and effective for modern talent management practices.

Next steps:

- What is the balance between standardization and customization in your talent management practice? Is there a better balance to be gained by skillfully improving standardization?

- To what practice or initiative could you apply the three principles of standardization (local needs, options, support)?

- Are there pockets of customization that are innovative and could be scaled up to benefit the whole organization or improve the current standard?

Your next move:

Challenge or rethink an old program, standard or not, that is crying out for purposeful abandonment.

24. PURPOSEFUL ABANDONMENT

Every new dance step reaches a peak of popularity. Some live on and are accepted by future generations. Some are quickly forgotten. The problem with talent management dance steps is that yesterday's routines are still around and may be past their prime. We need to stop going through the motions on some old practices that don't serve us well today and move on to something better.

"So are you going to kill this system or not?"

This question was repeatedly posed to me upon entering a new organization as the leader of learning and development. The system was an early attempt at an electronic talent management program. My initial response: "I don't know. Let me check into it."

> ## So much of what ends up as talent development driftwood starts out as good lumber.

My research in the ensuing weeks uncovered the heartache often felt with pioneering work in electronic talent management. It was ushered in with the promise of paperless administration, streamlined processes and revolutionary reporting available at your fingertips. The reporting capabilities were going to be so amazing that it would cause line management to immediately drop what they were doing and gaze admiringly at the strategic insight instantaneously produced by the system.

The reality was such a disappointment and drain on scarce resources that someone should have pulled the plug years earlier. It was clear that the department I now led was responsible for deciding the fate of this system.

As the new guy, it was an easy call to cut the old system and transition to something more promising. In fact, the honeymoon period for new leaders is often the time to clean up and start fresh. Now, years later, I wonder if my shop includes any programs or practices that deserve a similar fate?

Peter Drucker reportedly promoted a practice called purposeful abandonment. On an annual basis, an effective executive reviews the major practices and programs to determine if they are still serving their original purpose. Many of us, as we approach a new budget planning cycle, should consider purposeful abandonment for greater learning and development impact.

Why Drift?

So much of what ends up as talent development driftwood starts out as good lumber. The cause is right, the support is there and the material is promising. But even programs that start strong can end up adrift. Here are the signs that it is time for a program or process review:

- **Yes-to-everything:** This is the end result of working in a function that has a hard time saying no. Consider a typical corporate university: The initial offerings line up well with the mission. Then a new request comes in from an executive and another course is created. Teaching faculty lobby for sequel training to bring graduates back to cover the good material that didn't fit into the first class. Then, you translate the new business bestseller or fad into a blended program to show that your organization is on the cutting edge. Of course, you want it all and end up with an unfocused mess, vulnerable to the next round of budget cuts.

- **Overdone excellence:** This is the misapplication of continuous improvement. The new online module was well-received, so you go back and add new features because you think they'll like it even better. The current management training program is fine, but the new program manager wants to leave his mark, so the latest thinking on a semi-related topic is crammed into the curriculum. The class liked the executive lunch, so we'll add a breakfast and dinner encounter. You get the picture. In the end, our focus shifts from fulfilling the primary charter to chasing frills and peripheral features.

- **My old friend:** Work that should be up for review and revision remains stagnant because an emotional attachment keeps us from taking a harder look. While the program isn't hitting the mark anymore, the training has a historical significance. Perhaps it's a pet project that has received more resources than you care to tally but the end result still isn't satisfactory. You wait and hope improvement is right around the corner. The disappointing talent management system I faced early in my tenure was a perfect example of this substandard program.

Under Review

The trick to conducting a purposeful abandonment review is getting in the right frame of mind. Take the approach of an explorer rather than an accountant. Put on the hat of a new leader when reviewing ways to boost the performance and add value. It's often helpful to reaffirm the core purpose and utility of a program by getting feedback from people you would involve in focus groups and stakeholder interviews at the front end of program creation.

Swapfest is another useful exercise. With a group, brainstorm what you would do if you had 20 percent more resources to create new offerings, and alternatively, what you would do with 20 percent fewer resources. (For many of us, a 20 percent reduction can be more of an annual budget reality than a hypothetical exercise.) Swapping out low-value programs with new possibilities energizes and enables us to proactively create the future of learning.

Sometimes, drastic budget cuts and dramatic resource shifts cause us to examine the worth of the current suite of talent management programs. Better practitioners don't wait for circumstances to manage their renewal agendas but instead courageously examine the worth of their practices and initiatives. There is great benefit to revalidating the worth of a system or eliminating a suboptimal practice to free up time and resources for something innovative and new.

Next steps:

- Do you have a regular cycle or annual routine to examine the worth of your full set of talent management programs and initiatives?

- Do any of your current offerings look like "yes-to-everything," "overdone excellence" or "my old friend" programs that should be streamlined or eliminated?

- How can you creatively review your talent management portfolio as a way to create new programs and take courageous action on underperforming systems?

Your next move:
To better your chance at success, spend time honing your pitch for a new idea.

25. YOU'VE GOT TWO MINUTES

In most dance competitions, you can't get on the dance floor without a partner. In organizational life, the best partner for talent management is the CEO. Senior management commitment is often a prerequisite for a new development program to be successful. But beware: Time is short and the CEO is the most demanding partner, requiring your best even before the first steps are taken.

There are many exciting things about talent management, and sometimes that excitement can get us into trouble.

I remember my exhilaration years ago in going eyeball-to-eyeball with my CEO about a new talent management initiative. After a polite opening, it became clear that I had only two minutes to win him over.

Out went most of my 10-page deck covering the theory of the project, the cutting-edge innovation and the multi-layer change effort required. I had to quickly boil the message down to its essence. I sensed the outcome was either going to be a head nod — meaning he got it — or squinting eyes and a series of increasingly skeptical questions. I did make it out alive that day, but I will never forget the lesson from that two-minute drill: Clearly communicate that the need is real and the solution is practical.

As I reflect on why line leaders put a premium on the practical over the exciting, I realize that those who reflect or amplify the complexity of their ideas will not have influence. Our task is to add value with solutions that simplify, not pile on complexity.

Heading Into Trouble

Unfortunately, our enthusiasm for our own bright ideas can blind us to the test of practicality. So how do you know if you are headed for trouble? Here are four signs you aren't being practical:

1. You can't explain the core of your proposal in four minutes or less — or everything you are explaining is equally important and you can't

prioritize the critical elements. Or maybe the execution phase lacks much thinking at all.

2. The graphic flowchart of your initiative includes more than three boxes and three arrows. I refer to this as the "bad highway interchange" chart.

3. You build the solution around the award criteria for a professional society submission or making a magazine list. I was in a staff meeting recently when an HR department was requesting to add a new element to an already successful practice because a magazine had changed its "best of" ranking criteria.

4. It worked so well last time, you bring it back with add-ons, even though last time was just fine. You feel your department won't be respected if you don't bring something fresh and challenging.

> **The two-minute drill forced me to clearly communicate that the need was real and the solution was practical.**

The Clock Begins

Are you meeting with the CEO soon about your latest project that you believe will revolutionize the company? Before you walk into her office, let's check the practicality of your idea, minute by minute. The good news is the CEO is in a generous mood today and you'll be given four minutes of undivided attention.

- **First minute:** Is it real? Can you begin with a real business problem or opportunity that the CEO cares about?

- **Second minute:** Is it direct? Can you make a logical connection between the need and the solution you propose? Does it apply lean thinking by taking the most direct path to resolve the issue?

- **Third minute:** Is it familiar? Does your proposal balance familiar aspects with new thinking? Does the listener hear common business language or need a translator because you're using HR speak?

- **Fourth minute:** Is it well-planned? Without going into too much detail, can you show you've thought through the execution and sustaining essentials of your initiative? How will you overcome the potential obstacles?

- **Fifth minute:** Silence. Your four minutes are over. You've kept it crisp and are waiting for a response. You can tell she is thinking it over. Most likely, she is reflecting on your track record. Has your prior work been successful and impactful? If so, you will probably hear a yes. If not, scale back your proposal to a pilot test as a way to build confidence.

There is a growing list of complex and urgent talent management challenges. As leaders, our job is to strike the right balance in our solutions, avoiding oversimplification that underdelivers and complexity that overwhelms. Taking the time upfront to get it right will pay off, especially the next time you are faced with a two-minute drill.

Next steps:

- How can you practice more crisp communication and avoid HR speak when explaining talent management efforts?

- Do your presentations leave senior management with the belief that talent development ideas address real needs and provide practical solutions?

- When speaking about plans, do you build confidence in listeners that your new idea is well-researched with a strong focus on execution and results?

AFTERWORD

Over time, I believe star talent makes the greatest difference in organization performance. Winning performance can never be taken for granted, however, and the dance of nurturing and inspiring star talent is never-ending.

I hope these 25 ideas will help you and your organization in the journey to keep in step with the music of today and help your talent shine brightly tomorrow.

ABOUT THE AUTHOR

Kevin D. Wilde is vice president of organization effectiveness and chief learning officer at General Mills Inc., where he is responsible for worldwide people growth, including talent management, executive development and the company's leadership institute. Since he joined the company in 1998, General Mills has consistently been recognized for its development work. *Fortune* ranked the company as one of the best companies for leadership development and it has received *Training* Hall of Fame designation as a top company for employee development.

In 2007, *Chief Learning Officer* magazine selected Wilde as CLO of the Year. He is a columnist for *Talent Management* magazine and his work has been published in more than a dozen books, including *Coaching for Leadership* and the *Pfeiffer Annual: Leadership Development*. In 2011, his writing for *Talent Management* received a national award for editorial excellence from the American Society of Business Publication Editors. Before joining General Mills, Wilde spent 17 years at General Electric in human resources positions in the healthcare and capital divisions, as well as corporate assignments at GE's Crotonville management development center and positions in manufacturing, marketing and Six Sigma quality.

Wilde received a bachelor's degree in marketing and education from the University of Wisconsin at Stout in 1980 and a master's degree in administrative leadership and adult education from the University of Wisconsin at Milwaukee in 1981.

He can be found at www.kevinwildeonline.com.